# Little Book
## of
# LITTLE QUILTS

KATHARINE GUERRIER

Illustrated by Penny Brown

WATSON-GUPTILL PUBLICATIONS/NEW YORK

## Acknowledgments

Many thanks to all the talented quilting friends
who helped out with designing and stitching:
Eilean Macdonald, Sarah Fincken, Lynn Cooke, Helen Milosavljevich,
Stella White, Ngaire Brooks, Christine Porter, and Anne Tuck.

Heartfelt thanks and love to my husband George Hudson,
who took over all the household chores during
the production of this book.

Copyright © 1998 by MQ Publications, Ltd.
Text © 1998 by Katharine Guerrier
Illustrations © 1998 by Penny Brown

Published by MQ Publications, Ltd.,
254–258 Goswell Road, London EC1V 7EB
Editors: Ljiljana Baird and Simona Hill
Designer: Yvonne Dedman

First published in the United States in 1998
by Watson-Guptill Publications,
a division of BPI Communications, Inc.,
1515 Broadway, New York, N.Y. 10036

Library of Congress Catalog Card Number: 97-62555

ISBN 0-8230-2826-7

Printed in Italy

First printing, 1998

1 2 3 4 5 6 7 8 9 / 06 05 04 03 02 01 00 99 98

# Contents

# Introduction

What is it about small quilts that makes them so appealing?

When leisure time is at a premium in our busy lives, making small, quickly completed projects presents us with the ideal opportunity to try out many more quilts designs and techniques than might otherwise be possible. For some of us, particularly beginners, the considerable commitment and expense involved in making a full-size bed quilt often presents a daunting challenge. Small quilts offer the chance to experiment with color and design, to refine and develop techniques and ideas that one day may be incorporated into large-scale projects.

The development of the rotary cutting set has increased our ability to accurately cut small pieces of fabric, and this, combined with modern speed-piecing techniques, has made many traditional, time-honored designs more accessible. As well as promising more successful results, speed-piecing methods virtually eliminate the need to handle single tiny pieces of fabric.

The field of patchwork and quilting is wide-ranging and the choice of fabrics and designs often prove irresistible, such that many quilters often find their ideas rapidly overtake their allotment of available time needed to make all the quilts they have in mind.

*Opposite: A selection of some of the little quilts that this book shows you how to make—even a beginner could try these with confidence.*

# Template-free Quilts

With so many demands on our time, the creative opportunities afforded by quiltmaking can seem a luxury, but the availability of rotary cutting tools teamed with speed-piecing techniques makes it possible to construct quilts with ever-increasing speed and accuracy.

Many of the time-honored patterns—especially those that use simple shapes—can be made without templates and the time-consuming process of marking and cutting each individual piece with scissors.

By investing a little time and effort in learning to use a rotary cutting set and familiarizing yourself with the basics of quick-piecing, you will save many hours of cutting time in your future quiltmaking.

In this selection of template-free quilts, there is a range of designs and piecing methods. For the beginner, Quaker

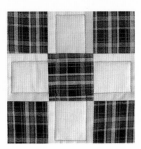

Kitchen and Rail Fence will provide easy practice. More challenging are Amish Triangles, Diamonds and Pinwheels, and Flying Geese. But, whatever your choice, if time is short, the techniques outlined in this chapter will make it possible.

# Flying Geese

Set in a medallion format, this small wallhanging makes novel use of the flying geese unit. To effectively distinguish the geese from the sky, mix prints with solids in coordinating colors.

Finished size: 28 x 28in/71 x 71cm
Skill level: Intermediate

## Materials

- Floral border print: ½yd/0.5m
- Leaf print for the geese: ¼yd/0.25m
- Red: ½yd/0.5m
- Grey for binding: ½yd/0.5m
- Backing: 30in/76cm square
- Batting: 30in/76cm square

- For quilting patterns see pages 136 and 137

## Cutting

1 From the leaf print, for the flying geese units, cut 18 squares 3¾in/9.5cm.

2 From red, for the flying geese units, cut 72 squares 2⅛in/5.5cm. For the sashing around the center units, cut two strips 5½ x 1½in/14 x 3.75cm and two strips 7½ x 1½in/19 x 3.75cm. Cut eight corner posts each 3in/7.5cm square. Cut four corner posts for the borders each 6in/15.25cm square.

3 Cut four borders 17½ x 6in/ 44.5 x 15.25cm.

## Flying Geese

The columns of flying geese units are made using the speed-piecing method below.

1 On the wrong side of each 2⅛in/5.5cm red square, draw a diagonal line joining opposite corners. Clip off the edges of two opposite corners.

2 On top of the right side of a leaf print square, place two small red squares diagonal line side up. Make sure the clipped edges meet at the center and the straight edges align with those of the leaf square. Pin.

3 Stitch ¼in/0.75cm to each side of the diagonal line. Cut in half along the drawn line.

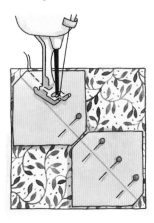

*fig 1*

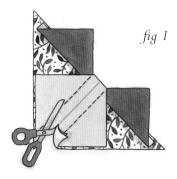

*fig 2*

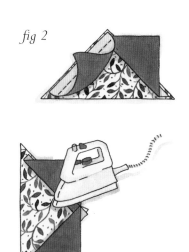

8 Press open and trim off the remaining seam allowances that project beyond the edges (*see figs 2 and 3*).

*fig 3*

4 Press the small triangles open.

5 Add a third and fourth red square, diagonal line up, to the remaining corners (*see fig 1*).

6 Stitch ¼in/0.75cm to each side of the line (*see fig 1*).

7 Cut in half along the diagonal line (*see fig 1*).

## Assembling the Quilt Top

1 For the quilt center, stitch together two sets of four flying geese units. Place the sets side by side so that the points lie in opposite directions. Stitch the sets together.

2 Stitch the shorter sashing to the top and bottom of the unit. Add the longer strips to each side.

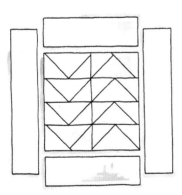

*Opposite: Detail of the flying geese units, two of the small quilted rosettes in the corner posts above the border, and the swirl pattern in the sashing around the center unit.*

3 Sew together four sets of six flying geese units.

4 Arrange these and four small corner posts (A) around the center panel so that the points of the flying geese flow anti-clockwise.

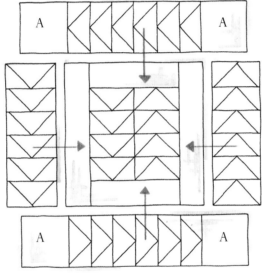

5 Stitch two flying geese units to opposite sides of the center panel.

6 Stitch two corner posts to each end of the remaining two geese units. Stitch to the top and bottom.

7 Stitch four sets of ten flying geese units together. Arrange the strips in a clockwise direction around the quilt center. Add four corner posts. Stitch the units in place as before.

## Finishing

1 Stitch one 6in/15.25cm corner post to each end of two borders. Stitch the short borders to opposite sides. Add the borders with corner posts to the remaining sides.

2 Transfer the rosette and curved border quilting designs to the quilt top—one large rosette in the four border corners, one small rosette in the corner posts, and the swirl pattern in the sashing around the center.

3 Make up the quilt sandwich, then hand quilt the design.

4 Machine quilt in-the-ditch in all the seams and around the flying geese units. On the outer borders quilt straight lines ¼in/0.75cm apart.

5 Cut and piece a length of binding 2½ x 118in/6.5 x 299cm.

6 Bind the quilt and miter the corners to finish.

# Pastel Crib Quilt

Pretty pastel prints in soft blues and pinks are offset
with pale plaids in this country-style crib quilt.
The unusual scalloped border adds to the overall delicacy
of the piece.

Finished size: 36 x 36in/91.5 x 91.5cm
Number of blocks: 16
Skill level: Confident beginner

## Materials

- Selection of floral and plaid
  fabric scraps in pale blue and
  pastel pink, each scrap to
  measure 8 x 4in/20.25 x 10cm
  —1yd/1m in total
- Blue and white plaid for the
  inner border and binding:
  ¾yd/0.75m
- Floral print for the outer
  border: ¾yd/0.75m
- Backing: 38in/97cm square
- Low-loft batting: 38in/97cm
  square

## Cutting

The quilt top is made up of 16
four-patch blocks or 64 half-
square triangles. Each four-patch
requires three different fabrics.

1 For each four-patch, from
one fabric, cut two squares
3⅞in/9.75cm. You will need 32
in total.

2 From each of two different
contrasting fabrics, cut 16
squares each 3⅞in/9.75cm—32
in total. Keep the fabrics for each
four-patch separate and label
them as you work to avoid
confusion.

3 For the inner border, cut
four strips each 2 x 27in/
5 x 68.75cm.

4 For the scalloped border,
cut four strips
3½ x 38in/9 x 96.5cm.

5 To make the
scallop, cut a strip
of paper 3 x 31in/
7.5 x 78.75cm. Trace
the scallop pattern
provided on page 15
onto the paper and cut
out the shape. Place
the paper pattern on
the border fabric. Pin
and cut out.

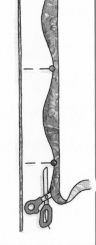

6 For the binding, cut and piece a length of bias binding 2½ x 145in/6.5 x 370cm long.

## Assembling the Four-patch Blocks

1 Pair up the four squares for each block, ensuring that each pair contains one square cut in step 1 of Cutting.

2 Draw a diagonal line joining two opposite corners on the wrong side of the lighter of the two fabrics.

3 Stitch ¼in/0.75cm from each side of the drawn line.

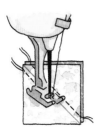

4 Cut along the drawn line to yield two bicolor half-square triangles.

5 Arrange the four squares into a four-patch block so that the outer triangles are the same fabric and the inner triangles are alternate prints.

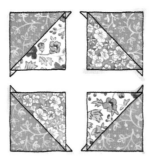

6 Stitch the squares together, first into pairs, then into the block. Make 15 more units.

7 Arrange the 16 blocks, four across and four down, alternating the color sequence. Stitch the blocks into rows. Stitch the rows together.

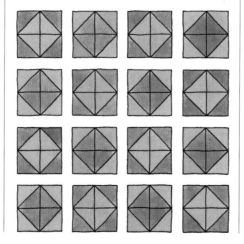

## Borders

1 Stitch plaid borders to opposite sides of the quilt top. Trim the excess. Press. Repeat to stitch borders across the top and bottom.

2 Trim the width of the inner border to 1½in/3.75cm.

3 Add the scalloped border and miter the corners following the instructions on page 131.

## Finishing

1 Make up the quilt sandwich following the instructions on page 132.

2 Baste a grid of 4in/10cm squares across the quilt top and around the outer edges.

3 Machine-quilt the blocks close to the vertical, horizontal, and diagonal seams.

4 Machine-quilt the inner border close to both seams and the outer border ¼in/ 0.75cm from the plaid.

*Opposite: Detail of a four-patch block, showing the pastel prints.*

5 To bind the quilt, the bias cut of the binding will enable you to gently ease the binding around the scalloped edges without creating puckers or distorting the fabric.

*Right:* Use the scallop border opposite to make a paper pattern. Trace the pattern opposite from the baseline to the broken line. Repeat and join the units together until the length measures 31in/78.75cm This will allow sufficient fabric to create a miter.

repeat

Scallop border
*pattern shown
actual size*

# Diamonds and Pinwheels

Diamonds and Pinwheels is a scrap quilt made from half-square triangles in a restricted palette of blue and beige. The overall unity of the design is created by using the same two fabrics for the pinwheel blocks.

Finished size: 42 x 42in/106.75 x 106.75cm
Number of blocks: 9
Finished block: 12 x 12in/30.5 x 30.5cm
Skill level: Intermediate

## Materials

- Navy blue for the pinwheels: ½yd/0.5m
- Light beige for the pinwheels: ½yd/0.5m
- Selection of blue fabric scraps each at least 4in/10cm square: ¾yd/0.75m in total
- Selection of light beige fabric scraps at least 4in/10cm square: ¾yd/0.75m in total
- Multicolored turquoise for the border and binding: ¾yd/0.75m
- 16 buttons
- Backing: 44in/1.2m square
- Batting: 44in/1.2m square

## Cutting

1 From navy, for the pinwheels, cut 32 squares each 3⅞in/9.75cm. Cut the same from light beige.

2 From scraps, cut 54 beige and 54 mixed blue squares 3⅞in/9.75 cm.

3 From the turquoise border fabric, cut twelve rectangles 6½ x 3½in/16.5 x 9cm.

4 For the binding, from turquoise, cut and piece a continuous length 2½in x 5yd/6.5 x 457cm.

## Making the Half-square Triangles for the Pinwheels

1 Pair up the light and dark squares into 32 units, right sides together.

2 On the wrong side of the lighter fabric, draw a diagonal line joining two corners.

3 Machine-stitch ¼in/0.75cm to each side of the line.

4 Cut along each pencil line to yield 64 half-square triangles. Press the seams toward the darker fabric.

5 Repeat steps 1–4 above to make 108 half-square triangles using the beige and mixed blue squares.

## Making the Blocks

1 Arrange twelve beige and mixed blue half-square triangles, and four navy and light beige half-square triangles into the light and dark diamond configuration below.

2 Following the arrangement, sew four units into a row. Stitch four rows together to make a block.

3 Make nine blocks, then arrange the blocks into three rows of three.

4 Stitch the blocks into rows. Stitch the rows together.

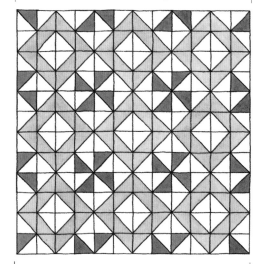

## Border

1 Using the remaining half-square triangles and the twelve turquoise rectangles, arrange the pieces into two sets of two borders as shown in the illustrations below. Stitch the units together. Press the seams open.

2 Stitch each shorter border to the quilt top and bottom, aligning all seams.

3 Stitch the longer borders to the sides.

## Finishing

1 Assemble the quilt sandwich. Baste a 4in/10cm grid across the quilt top, then baste around the raw edges.

2 Using invisible thread, machine- or handquilt in-the-ditch along the seams separating the blocks, and around the diamonds for definition.

3 Tie-quilt the center of the pinwheels by stitching a button to the center of each using embroidery thread and a decorative knot. (see page 27)

4 Trim the backing and batting even with the dimensions of the quilt top.

5 Bind the quilt following the instructions on page 133. Miter the corners.

# Quaker Kitchen

Alternate blocks made of simple squares
and rectangles make a small wallhanging suitable for
a country-style kitchen.

Finished size: 28 x 22in/71 x 56cm
Number of blocks: 12
Finished block: 6½ x 6½in/16.5 x 16.5cm
Skill level: Beginner

## Materials

- Plaid A: ¼yd/0.25m square
- Plaid B: ¼yd/0.25m square
- Plaid C: ¼yd/0.25m square
- Coffee D: ¼yd/0.25m square
- Cream E: ¼yd/0.25m square
- Navy blue F: ¼yd/0.25m
- Maroon G: ¼yd/0.25m square
- Backing: 30 x 24in/76 x 61cm
- Batting: 30 x 24in/76 x 61cm

## Cutting

**1** From A, for the nine-patch blocks, cut 20 squares each 2½in/6.5cm.

**2** From B, for the nine-patch blocks, cut eight squares each 2½in/6.5cm.

**3** From C, for the rectangle blocks, cut six pieces 6½ x 2½in/16.5 x 6.5cm. For the inner border, cut two strips 12½ x 1½in/31.75 x 3.75cm. Cut two strips 10½ x 1½in/26.75 x 3.75cm.

**4** From D, for the nine-patch blocks, cut 16 squares each 2½in/6.5cm.

**5** From E, for the rectangle blocks, cut six pieces 6½ x 2½in/16.5 x 6.5cm. For the inner border, cut two strips 12½ x 1½in/31.75 x 3.75cm. Cut two strips 10½ x 1½in/26.75 x 3.75cm.

**6** From F, for the nine-patch blocks, cut ten squares 2½in/6.5cm. For the rectangles, cut six pieces 6½ x 2½in/16.5 x 6.5cm. For the binding, cut and piece a length 106 x 2½in/270 x 6.5cm.

**7** From G, for the outside border, cut two strips 22½ x 1½in/57.25 x 3.75cm. Cut two strips 26½ x 1½in/67.25 x 3.75cm.

## Assembling the Blocks

Use ¼in/0.75cm seams.

1 Using the quilt plan, arrange each of the pieces on a clean, flat surface.

|   |   |   | F | B | F |   |   |   |
|---|---|---|---|---|---|---|---|---|
| E | C | F | B | F | B | E | C | F |
|   |   |   | F | B | F |   |   |   |
| A | D | A |   | E |   | A | D | A |
| D | A | D |   | C |   | D | A | D |
| A | D | A |   | F |   | A | D | A |
|   |   |   | F | B | F |   |   |   |
| E | C | F | B | F | B | E | C | F |
|   |   |   | F | B | F |   |   |   |
| A | D | A |   | E |   | A | D | A |
| D | A | D |   | C |   | D | A | D |
| A | D | A |   | F |   | A | D | A |

2 To make the nine-patch blocks, stitch three sets of three squares together into vertical columns of three.

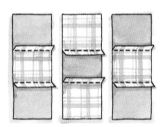

3 Press the seams toward the outer blocks on the outer rows and toward the center block on the middle row. This makes the seams interlock when the rows are stitched together and makes the joins stronger and more accurate.

4 Stitch the columns together.

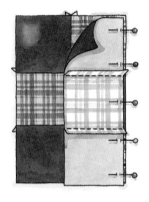

5 To make the rectangle blocks, stitch together three pieces for each block along the 6½in/16.5cm edge.

6 Stitch the blocks together into horizontal rows. Stitch the rows together.

## Borders

1 To make the inner border, stitch each 10½in/26.75cm C strip to a same-size E strip at the short end. Repeat with the 12½in/31.75cm strips.

2 Arrange the inner border pieces around the quilt top, alternating the colors. Stitch on the side borders first, then top and bottom borders.

3 Add the outer border in the same sequence.

## Finishing

1 Make up the quilt sandwich by spreading the backing right side down on a clean, flat surface. Center the batting on top, then the quilt top right side up and smooth out any wrinkles.

2 Baste a 4in/10cm grid through all the layers and around the edges.

3 Quilt in-the-ditch along the main seam lines separating the blocks.

4 Contour quilt within the squares and rectangles of each block and border.

5 Add separate continuous binding following the instructions on page 133.

# Amish Triangles

The color scheme of saturated purple, green, and eggplant
with highlights of lighter and brighter hues is
inspired by the distinctive Amish quilts.
The method teaches speed-piecing quarter-square triangles,
prominent in many traditional quilt designs.

Finished size: 30 x 30in/76 x 76 cm
Number of blocks: 9
Finished block: 8¼ x 8¼in/21 x 21cm
Skill level: Confident intermediate

## Materials

- 36 different solid color squares
  each 5in/13cm
- Green: ½yd/0.5m square
- Blue-grey: ½yd/0.5m square
- Purple: ½yd/0.5m square
- Eggplant: ¾yd/0.75m
- Batting: 32in/81cm square
- Backing: 32in/81cm square

## Cutting

1 Cut 36 squares 3½in/9cm.
From the remainder, for the
highlights in the binding, cut strips
1¼ x 2½in/3 x 6.5cm.

2 For the sashing, from green,
blue-grey, purple, and
eggplant, cut strips 1½in/3.75cm
wide across the width of the
fabric. Cut each as you need it.

3 For the quilt border, from
eggplant, cut strips 3in/
7.5cm wide across the width of
the fabric.

4 For the binding, from
eggplant, cut strips to make
a length 2½ x 124in/6.5 x
315cm.

## Assembling the Blocks

1 With right sides together,
pair up the squares.

2 On the reverse of the lightest
fabric, draw diagonal lines,
joining the corners. Stitch ¼in/
0.75cm to the right of the drawn
line, from the outer edge to the
center point only.

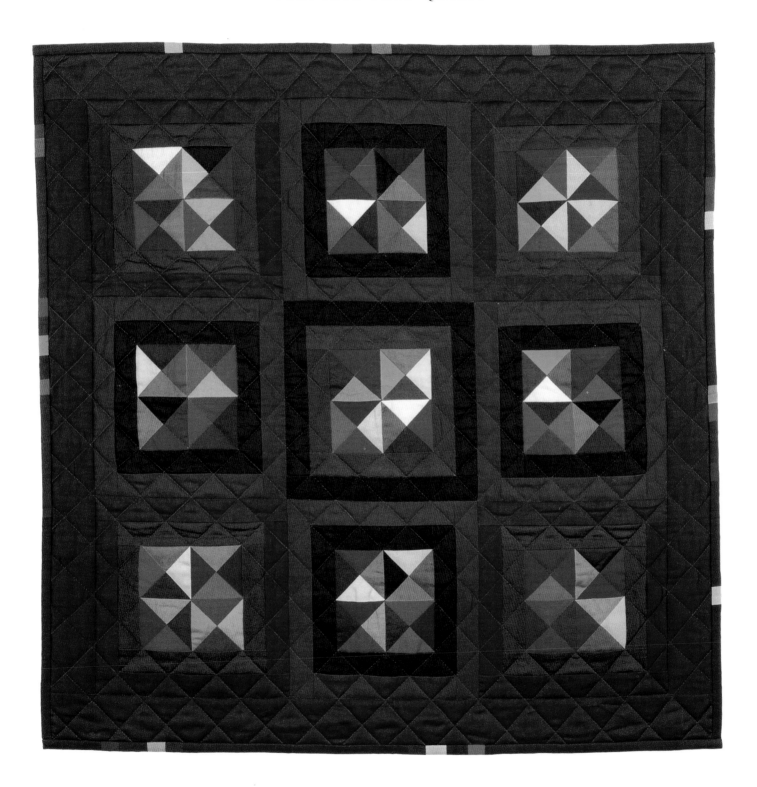

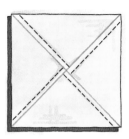

3 Cut along the drawn lines to yield four bicolor triangular units.

4 Repeat with the remaining squares. Press each open.

5 Pair each bicolor unit with another unit of a different color. Stitch the units into squares. Press

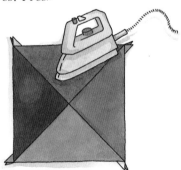

6 Stitch four squares into a block.

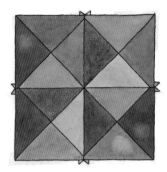

## Assembling the Quilt Top

1 To add the inner block sashing, stitch a blue-grey strip to the top and bottom of five blocks, trimming to fit as required. Add a sashing strip to each side.

2 To the remaining four blocks stitch green sashing.

3 To four of the blocks with blue-grey sashing, add an eggplant sashing, following the sequence above. These blocks form the four corners.

4 To the remaining block with blue-grey sashing, for the quilt center, stitch strips of green sashing.

5 To the remaining blocks stitch purple sashing.

6 Arrange the blocks into three rows of three.

7 Stitch the blocks into rows. Stitch the rows together.

## Finishing

1 Add the eggplant border to the quilt top and bottom then the sides. Trim each border to size. Press.

2 Mark diagonal quilting lines across the surface of the quilt to the edges.

3 Assemble the quilt sandwich and baste a 4in/10cm vertical and horizontal grid.

4 Quilt in-the-ditch around the outer block borders. Quilt the diagonal marked lines.

5 Trim the backing and batting even with the quilt top.

6 Make up the binding, adding the solid color strips at random intervals. Bind the quilt following the instructions on page 133. Miter the corners.

# Rail Fence

This variation of a traditional design is quick and easy to make using two simple blocks—speed-pieced half-square triangles and strip-pieced blocks.

Finished size: 28½ x 33in/72.5 x 83.75cm
Number of blocks: 42
Finished block: 4½ x 4½in/11.5 x 11.5cm
Skill level: Beginner

## Materials

- Green: ½yd/0.5m
- Yellow: ½yd/0.5m
- Purple: ½yd/0.5m
- Batting: 29 x 33in/74 x 84cm
- Backing: 29 x 33in/74 x 84cm
- Embroidery thread for tie-quilting

## Cutting

1 For the strip-pieced blocks, from green, cut five strips 2in/5cm wide across the full width of the fabric.

2 Cut the same from yellow and from purple.

3 For the half-square triangles, from green, cut five squares 5⅜in/13.5cm.

4 Cut the same from yellow.

## Strip-pieced Blocks and Half-square Triangles

1 Arrange the yellow, green, and purple strips into five sets of three strips. Sew three strips together along the long edge for each set. Press.

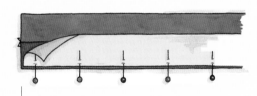

2 Cross-cut the strips at 5in/12.75cm intervals. Cut 33.

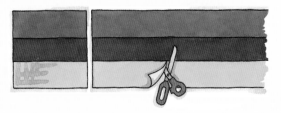

3 Make nine squares, following the instructions for piecing half-square triangles on page 14. One block will be leftover.

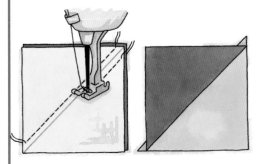

**Assembling the Quilt Top**

1 Using the photograph on page 26 as a guide, arrange the 42 blocks into the quilt top— six across and seven down. Ensure that the orientation of each block is correct.

2 Stitch the blocks into rows. Then stitch the rows together. Press.

3 Make up the quilt sandwich. Baste a vertical and horizontal grid 4in/10cm apart.

4 Tie a reef knot at the intersection of each block using embroidery thread. With the quilt top right side up, stab stitch through all the quilt layers.

Leave a long thread end without any knots. Bring the needle back through to the front 1/8in/0.5cm away from the first stitch. Make another stitch over the first and second stitches.

*Above: Half-square triangles and strip-pieced blocks, showing the reef knots at the block intersections.*

5 Tie a square knot, right over left, then left over right. Cut the thread ends to the required finished length.

6 From scraps, cut and piece four lengths of binding, 2½in/6.5cm wide, to fit the width and length of the quilt. Bind to finish. (see page 133)

# Foundation Piecing

One way to achieve a high degree of accuracy when piecing small blocks is to stitch them to a foundation fabric, onto which the block pattern has been drawn or stamped. The idea of stitching blocks to a foundation is not new: Log Cabin and crazy quilt patchwork are common traditional examples of this method of construction.

The difference with the method used in the projects in this chapter is that the design lines are drawn first onto the  foundation. This method allows exact piecing and planning, unlike crazy quilt patchwork, which has a more random and spontaneous approach.

The fabric pieces are pinned to the unmarked side of the foundation and the stitching is worked from the back of the block over the pre-drawn line. The results look impressive because of the tiny pieces of fabric used. However, it is a relatively easy technique, which will produce appealing and accurate results even for beginners. Each block is worked separately, allowing plenty of opportunity to rearrange the configuration of units according to individual preference.

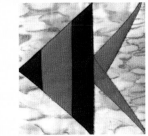

# Log Cabin Barn Raising

Use up your fabric scraps with this Log Cabin variation. The plain red center square is surrounded by strips of small-patterned fabric in contrasting light and dark values.

Finished size: 20 x 20in/50.75 x 50.75cm
Number of blocks: 36
Finished block: 3 x 3in/7.5 x 7.5cm
Skill level: Intermediate

## Materials

- Plain white muslin for the foundations: ¾yd/0.75m
- Red for the centers: 15in/38cm square
- Light and dark fabric scraps in small prints, checks, polka dots, florals, and geometric patterns: each at least 1 x 3½in/2.5 x 9cm
- Backing: 22in/61cm square
- Binding: ¼yd/0.25m
- Iron-on transfer pencil
- Tracing paper

- For template see page 135

## Cutting

**1** For the foundation from plain white muslin, cut 36 squares each 4in/10cm.

**2** From red, cut 36 squares each 1in/2.5cm.

**3** From fabric scraps, cut strips 1 x 3½in/2.5 x 9cm, for the largest logs. There are 432 logs altogether. Sort the strips into light and dark values.

**4** For the border, cut 24 strips each 2 x 3½in/5 x 9cm. Cut four corner squares each 2in/5cm.

**5** For the binding, cut and piece strips 2½ x 90in/6.5 x 229cm in total.

## Making the Blocks

Use ¼in/0.75cm seams.

**1** To prepare the foundation squares, first trace the template provided using an iron-on transfer pencil and tracing paper. Then, following the manufacturer's instructions for the pencil, transfer the design onto each of the 36 foundation squares. The traced lines are your stitching lines.

2 On the reverse side of the traced lines, place a red square right side up so that it covers the center square completely. Hold the foundation fabric up to the light if you cannot see the traced lines through the fabric. Pin in place.

3 For each block you will need three light and three dark color logs. Follow the stitching order given on the template.

4 Begin with a light fabric. Cut a log long enough to cover the first drawn log, adding ¼in/0.75cm to each end. With right sides together, place the light fabric on the red square so that raw edges align. Pin.

5 Turn the foundation square over and sew on the traced line joining the first log to the red square. Begin and end at least two stitches beyond each seam. Fasten off with backstitch.

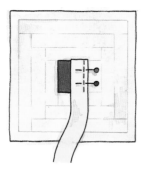

6 Turn the foundation over and trim away any excess fabric from the seam allowances and from each end. Press the log out flat.

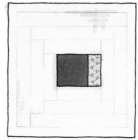

7 Using the same fabric, cut a second log and place it right side down on the red square so that it covers the end of the first log.

8 Turn the foundation fabric over to the traced lines and stitch on the line joining the two together. Trim the bulky seam and press the log out flat. Add logs 3 and 4 in the same way using dark fabric.

9 Continue to add logs, working around the red central square and retaining the light and dark color sequence.

10 For the final round, ensure the strips are wide enough to allow a ¼in/0.75cm seam at the outer edges, for use when joining the blocks together.

11 Make 35 more blocks in the same way.

## Making the Quilt Top

1 Stitch blocks into pairs, then into fours, then three blocks of six. Stitch the three horizontal rows together. Use the photograph as a guide to the position of light and dark logs.

2 To add the border, stitch together six strips for each of four sides.

3 Stitch a corner square to each end of two borders.

4 Add a muslin backing to the wrong side of each border, to equalize the weight of the blocks in the quilt center.

5 Stitch the two shorter borders to the quilt sides. Stitch the longer borders to the two remaining sides.

## Finishing

1 Follow the instructions on page 132 for making up the quilt sandwich. No batting is necessary for this quilt.

2 Machine-quilt the design along the horizontal and vertical grid of blocks and diagonally in both directions across each corner. Quilt in-the-ditch where the border meets the blocks.

3 Add the binding following the instructions on page 133 for mitered corners using continuous binding.

*Below: Detail of Log Cabin block.*

# Plain Sailing

Miniature blocks depicting beach huts and sailing ships set into a landscape of sea, sky, and beach evoke an idyllic seaside retreat. The design for Plain Sailing is made using the same principles as Log Cabin Barn Raising.

Finished size: 12¼ x 14½in/31 x 36.75cm
Number of blocks: 15

## Materials

- Lightweight muslin: ½yd/0.5m
- Sea fabric: ½yd/0.5m
- Sky fabric: ¼yd/0.25m
- Beach fabric: ¼yd/0.25m
- Scraps of cotton in bright colors, stripes, and checks for the sail boats and beach huts
- Backing: 15 x 17in/ 38 x 43cm
- Binding: ¼yd/0.25m
- Iron-on transfer pencil
- Tracing paper

- For templates see pages 134–5

## Cutting

1 From muslin, for the block foundations, cut nine squares each 4in/10cm.

2 Use an iron-on transfer pencil and tracing paper to trace each beach hut and sailing ship block from the templates provided. Transfer the design to the muslin following the manufacturer's instructions for using the pencil.

A = 1⅛ x 11½in/3 x 29.25cm
B = 2⅞ x 2⅝in/7.25 x 6.75cm
C = 2⅞ x 2⅞in/7.25 x 7.25cm
D = 2⅞ x 2⅞in/7.25 x 7.25cm
E = 2⅞ x 2⅞in/7.25 x 7.25cm
F = 2¼ x 11½in/5.75 x 29.25cm
G = 2⅞ x 1⅝in/7.25 x 4.25cm

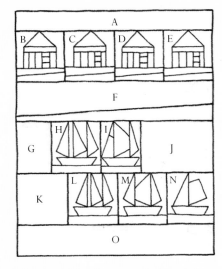

H = 2⅞ x 2⅞in/7.25 x 7.25cm
I = 2⅞ x 2⅜in/7.25 x 6cm
J = 2⅞ x 4½in/7.25 x 11.5cm
K = 2⅞ x 3in/7.25 x 7.5cm
L = 2⅞ x 2⅞in/7.25 x 7.25cm
M = 2⅞ x 2¾in/7.25 x 7cm
N = 2⅞ x 2½in/7.25 x 6.5cm
O = 1¾ x 11½in/4.5 x 29.25cm

3 Make templates for the ships, hut roof, and triangular blocks of sky at each side of the roof.

4 Place the templates right side down on the wrong side of appropriate fabric and cut out each shape, allowing ¼in/0.75cm seams all around. Making templates for awkward shapes ensures greater control over the direction of stripes and checks.

5 For the beach huts, from fabric scraps, cut strips at least 1in/2.5cm wide and 2in/5cm long.

6 For the beach and the sky, at each side of the block, cut strips 1 x 3½in/2.5 x 9cm.

7 For the binding, cut two strips 2 x 13in/5 x 33cm and two strips 2 x 16in/5 x 40.5cm.

**Assembling the Blocks**

1 To assemble the beach hut blocks, turn the foundation fabric over to the side you have not drawn on and place the window fabric right side up over the position of the center square. Hold the muslin up to the light to ensure the placement is accurate. The window should overlap the drawn square at each side. Pin in position.

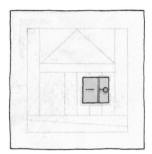

2 Follow the number guides on the template and place strip 2 over the window with right sides together and raw edges aligned. Pin the two together so

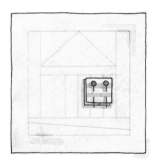

that the pieces do not shift. Turn the foundation fabric over and stitch on the line joining the window to strip 2. Sew a few extra stitches at each side to hold. Turn back and trim away the excess fabric from the seam to reduce bulk and trim each short end of the strip. Open out strip 2 and press flat.

3 Stitch strip 3 to the opposite side of the window in the same way. Add strips 4 and 5 to the two remaining sides. Continue to build up the beach hut design following the number guides. When the final pieces are added to each outer edge, ensure that the strips are sufficiently wide to allow for a ¼in/0.75cm seam to join the blocks together.

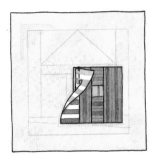

4 Make four beach huts and five sailing ship blocks in this way. Trim the excess foundation to ¼in/0.75cm all around the outer solid line.

## Assembling the Quilt Top

1 To make up the picture, using the remaining sky, beach, and sea fabric, compose your own seaside quilt by sewing the pieced blocks together and combining them with strips and rectangles of appropriate fabric.

2 Stitch horizontal rows of blocks together. Use the remaining muslin to back these extra pieces to equalize the weight of the quilt. Press the joining seams open to achieve the flattest effect.

## Finishing

1 Follow the instructions on page 132 for making up a quilt sandwich. No batting is necessary because the muslin will add sufficient weight.

2 Hand- or machine-quilt the design to represent the motion of the sea and sky.

3 Add the binding following the instructions on page 133.

*Above: Detail of beach huts.*
*Opposite: Detail of sailing ships.*

# Snail Trail

Blocks made of simple squares and triangles create the illusion of spirals and curved seams and are deceptively easy to make. The secret is in the clever placement of dark and light values within each block. Try rearranging the blocks before stitching them together to create different optical configurations.

Finished size: 14 x 14in/35.5 x 35.5cm
Number of blocks: 9
Finished block: 3 x 3in/7.5 x 7.5cm
Skill level: Intermediate

## Materials

- Lightweight muslin for the foundation: ½yd/0.5m
- A good selection of fabric scraps in light and dark values, at least 3in/7.5cm square for the blocks and 12 x 1in/ 30 x 2.5cm for the borders
- Binding: ¼yd/0.25m
- Backing: 16in/41cm square
- Iron-on transfer pencil
- Tracing paper

- For template see page 135

## Cutting

1 For the center four-patch, cut three light strips 1 x 7in/ 2.5 x 17.75cm. Cut three dark strips the same size.

2 For the block foundations, from muslin, cut nine squares 4in/10cm.

3 To line the inner border, cut four muslin strips 1½ x 10½in/ 3.75 x 26.75cm.

4 Using a transfer pencil, and following the manufacturer's instructions, transfer the template to the center of each foundation.

5 For the inner border, cut four strips 1½ x 10½in/3.75 x 26.75cm.

6 For the striped border, cut 19 dark strips 1 x 12in/2.5 x 30.5cm.

7 From dark scraps, cut four corners 2½in/6.5cm square.

8 For the binding, cut and piece a length 2½ x 65in/ 6.5 x 165cm.

## Assembling the Snail Trail Block

1 For the center four-patch, place one light and one dark strip right sides together. Stitch along one long edge. Press. Cut into 1in/2.5cm strips across both fabrics. Repeat with the remaining strips. Cut six from each set.

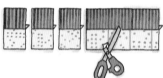

2 Stitch two segments together to make a four-patch. Match center points and alternate the colors. Press.

3 Put a pin through the seam at the center of the four-patch and match this to the center of the plain side of the muslin block. If the line drawing is not visible through the muslin, tape the square to a window and draw over the lines with a sharp pencil.

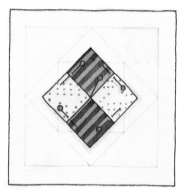

4 Pin the four-patch to the foundation right side up, aligning the seams with the pattern below.

5 Note the position of the light and dark fabrics. Cut a piece of light fabric to adequately cover area L1. Pin right side down over the four-patch, so that raw edges are aligned.

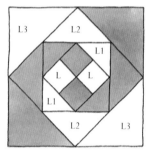

6 Turn the foundation square over and sew along the seam line joining L1 to the four-patch. Make one or two extra stitches at each end to secure.

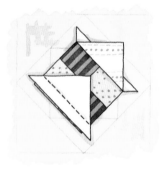

*Left: Detail of Snail Trail block.*

7 Turn the foundation over and trim away any excess fabric from the seam allowance.

8 Flip the piece over and press flat to the foundation.

9 Repeat, stitching a second light piece opposite the first.

10 Add dark patches to the remaining opposite sides.

11 Repeat for round two. For the final round, cut the light and dark pieces large enough to extend ¼in/0.75cm beyond the outer drawn lines. This will provide a seam to join the completed blocks together.

12 Add the final round following the key as a guide to color placement. Make nine blocks in total.

13 Press the blocks and place foundation side up. Trim the foundation back to ¼in/0.75cm beyond the outer solid line.

14 Arrange the nine blocks into three rows of three. Stitch the blocks into separate rows and press the seams flat. Join the three rows together.

## Borders

1 Line each inner border with a same-size foundation border and pin the two together. Stitch the inner border to the top and bottom of the quilt center. Stitch borders to the sides. Press. Trim to ¾in/2cm wide.

2 To make the striped border, stitch the 19 dark strips together along the long edge. Press the seams open.

3 Rule a line across the pieced fabric at one end and trim the edges.

4 Cross-cut the pieced fabric to yield four striped borders 2½in/6.5cm wide.

5 Cut strips of muslin to line the borders and baste. Stitch two pieced borders to opposite sides of the quilt. To each end of the remaining two pieced borders, stitch a 2½in/6.5cm square.

6 Stitch the border strips to the two remaining sides of the quilt top. Press.

7 Pin the backing to the wrong side of the quilt top.

8 Machine quilt in-the-ditch between the blocks, across the diagonal lines and along the inner border seams.

9 Trim the backing level with the quilt top. Bind with double-fold binding and miter the corners (*see page 131*).

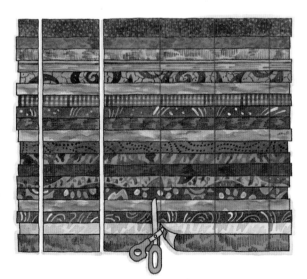

*Right: Border detail.*

# Roman Stripe

This Roman Stripe quilt, which uses bright solid colors set against a black ground, makes a strong graphic and visual statement. The regular repetition of the block is counteracted by the random arrangement of colored strips within each block.
The foundation used here is a tearaway stabilizer that is removed before the quilt sandwich is made up.

Finished size: 16 x 13½/40.5 x 34.25cm
Number of blocks: 12
Finished block: 3 x 3in/7.5 x 7.5cm
Skill level: Confident beginner

## Materials

- Selection of solid colors for blocks: 5in/12.75cm square
- Solid red, turquoise, lavender, and burgundy for the border: ¼yd/0.25m of each
- Black: ¼yd/0.25m
- Tearaway stabilizer: 15 x 20in/ 38 x 51cm
- Binding: ¼yd/0.25m
- Low-loft batting: 14 x 16in/ 36 x 41cm

- For template see page 135

## Cutting

1 From black, cut six squares 4½in/11.5cm. Cut each square in half across one diagonal to yield twelve triangles for one half of the block.

2 From the tearaway stabilizer, cut twelve squares each 4½in/11.5cm.

3 Trace the block design onto the twelve squares of tearaway stabilizer.

4 For the border, cut strips of red, turquoise, lavender, and burgundy 1½in/3.75cm wide across the width of the fabric.

5 For the diagonal strips, cut each as you need it.

## Assembling the Blocks

1 From a bright-colored solid, cut a triangle large enough to cover the dimensions of corner piece 1.

2 On the unprinted side of the stabilizer, place the piece right side up over the corner. Pin to secure.

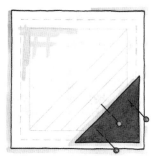

3 Cut a different color strip of fabric larger than the second area to be covered. Place this piece right side down over the first triangle, covering the drawn seam line and with raw edges aligned. Pin.

4 Turn the block over and sew on the first line, making a few extra stitches at each end of the line.

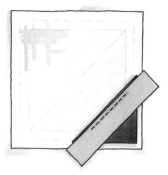

5 Flip the block over and trim away any excess fabric from the seam line. Press the pieces out flat.

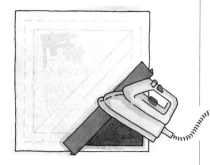

6 Continue cutting and adding pieces to cover the striped half of the block.

7 Add a black triangle to complete the block. Press.

8 Trim each completed block on the outer broken line. Carefully remove the tearaway stabilizer.

9 Follow steps 1–8 and make another eleven blocks.

10 Stitch the blocks into rows of three, then stitch the four rows together to make the quilt top.

## Borders

1 Stitch a red border to each side of the quilt. Trim the excess fabric from the top and bottom. Trim the width to ¾in/2cm and press open. Stitch a red border across the top and bottom, then trim and press in the same way.

2 Add a turquoise, lavender, and burgundy border in the same way.

3 Make up the quilt sandwich. Baste a horizontal and vertical grid across the quilt top.

4 Using invisible thread, quilt diagonal lines across the blocks using the stripes as a guide. Quilt close to the border seams.

5 Bind the raw edges with green (*see page 133*).

# Log Cabin Twist

Another variation of the Log Cabin design, this quilt creates the illusion of curved lines and rotating shapes by effectively manipulating fabric into inset angles.

Finished size: 23 x 23in/58.5 x 58.5cm
Number of blocks: 9
Finished block: 3 x 3in/7.5 x 7.5cm
Skill level: Intermediate

## Materials

♦ Blue: ½yd/0.5m
♦ Green: ½yd/0.5m
♦ Scraps of tearaway stabilizer
♦ Batting: 25in/64cm square
♦ Backing: 25in/64cm square

♦ For template see page 136

## Preparing the Foundation

1 From tearaway stabilizer, cut nine squares each 4½in/ 11.5cm.

2 Transfer the block diagram onto each square. Include the broken line around the edge.

3 For the inner border, from green, cut one strip 2½ x 9½in/6.5 x 24cm, and one strip 2½ x 13½in/6.5 x 34.25cm. Cut the same from blue.

4 For the outer border, from green, cut one strip 15½ x 13½in/39.5 x 34.25cm and one strip 15½ x 23½in/39.5 x 59.75cm.

5 Cut each fabric piece as you require it.

6 For the binding, from green, cut two strips, 2½ x 25in/ 6.5 x 63.5cm. Cut the same from blue.

## Making the Blocks

1 For the center, cut a square of green slightly larger than the dimensions on the pattern. Pin in place, right side up, on the unprinted side of the stabilizer.

2 Cut two strips of blue large enough to cover the areas marked 2, plus seam allowances. (Any excess will be trimmed away as the block is stitched.)

3 Pin the blue fabric pieces to opposite sides of the green square, right side down and with raw edges aligned.

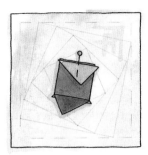

4 Turn the whole block over. Stitch the pieces in place on the seam line joining area 1 to areas 2. Continue stitching two or three stitches beyond the seam line.

*Below: Detail of one block.*

5 Turn the block back over and trim away any excess fabric. Press the fabric pieces out flat.

6 Continue adding strips, following the correct color sequence, until the block is complete. The last round of strips must be wide enough to cover the outer broken line on each of the four sides.

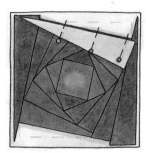

## Assembling the Quilt Top

1 Arrange the nine blocks into the quilt top. Stitch the blocks together into three rows of three. Stitch the rows together.

2 Add the short green inner border to the quilt top and the short blue border to the bottom. Stitch the last green inner border to the right-hand side of the quilt and the blue inner border to the left-hand side. Trim the quilt square.

3 Add the shorter blue outer border to the quilt top, and the shorter green outer border to the bottom. Add the longer green border to the left-hand side and the remaining border to the right-hand side. Trim the quilt square. Carefully remove the stabilizer.

4 Make up the quilt sandwich. Baste a grid 4in/10cm apart.

5 Using invisible thread and referring to the photograph as a guide, quilt the grid pattern across the quilt surface.

6 Bind the quilt with separate binding following the instructions on page 133 of the Techniques chapter.

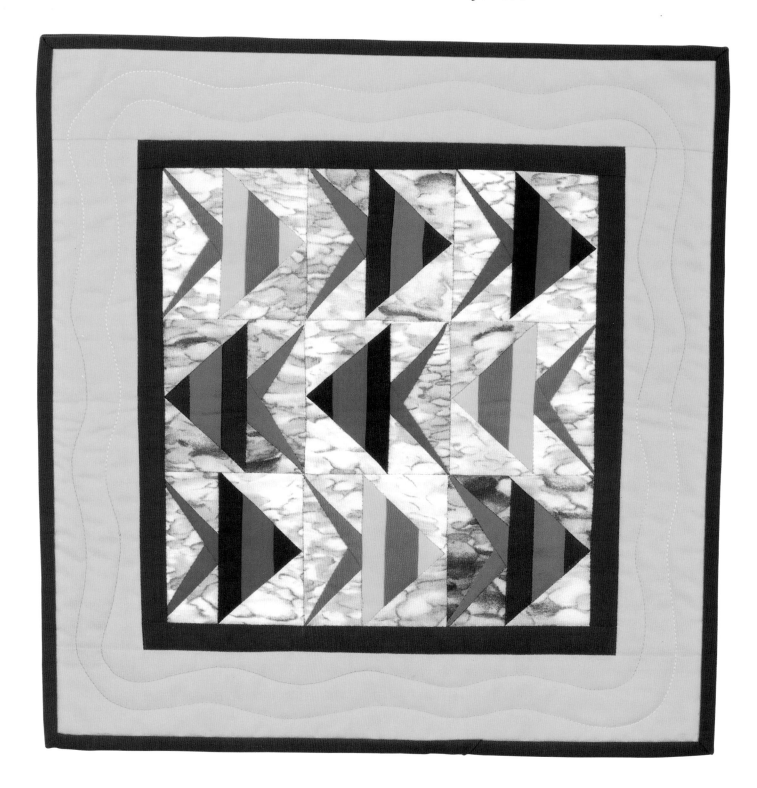

# Tropical Fish

These tropical fish are stitched to a tearaway stabilizer foundation instead of a muslin foundation. Once stitched, the foundation is torn away.

Finished size: 14 x 14in/35.5 x 35.5cm
Number of blocks: 9
Finished block: 3 x 3in/7.5 x 7.5cm
Skill level: Intermediate

## Materials

- Selection of bright, solid-color fabric scraps for the fish—these are often available as charm packs in 5in/12.75cm squares
- Blue print for the water: ¼yd/0.25m
- Yellow for the border: ¼yd/0.25m
- Purple for the border and binding: ¼yd/0.25m
- Scraps of tearaway stabilizer
- Low-loft batting: 16in/41cm square
- Backing: 16in/41cm square

- For template see page 136

## Cutting

1 On the tearaway stabilizer, draw nine squares 4½in/ 11.5cm. Cut each out. Trace the fish design, with the broken outer line, onto each.

2 Cut the fabric pieces for the fish as they are required.

3 From purple, cut two inner borders 9¼ x 1in/23.5 x 2.5cm and two borders 10 x 1in/25.5 x 2.5cm.

4 From purple, cut and piece a length of binding 2½ x 64in/ 6.5 x 163cm.

5 From yellow, cut two outer borders 10½ x 2¼in/26.75 x 5.75cm, and two borders 13¾ x 2¼in/35 x 5.75cm.

## Making the Blocks

1 Cut a triangle of sea fabric to cover area 1 and extend beyond the broken line.

2 Place the fabric right side up on the unprinted side of the foundation, over area 1. Pin.

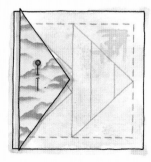

3 Cut a solid-color strip to cover area 2—the first part of the fish tail—large enough to allow for turnings.

4 Place the second piece of fabric right side down against the first piece and pin in place.

5 Turn the whole block over so that the diagram is visible.

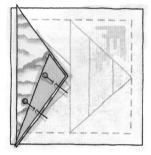

6 Stitch along the line joining area 1 to area 2. Begin and end two or three stitches beyond both ends of the seam.

*Right: Detail of the fish.*

7 Turn the block back over and trim away any excess seam allowance. Flip piece 2 over and press flat.

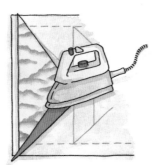

8 In the same way add strips for areas 3–10.

9 Trim each completed block on the outer dotted lines.

10 Make nine blocks, using three color schemes.

## Assembling the Quilt Top

1 Arrange the nine blocks, three across and three down, to make the quilt top.

2 Stitch the blocks into rows, then stitch the rows together, aligning seams.

3 Remove the tearaway stabilizer, ensuring that the stitching does not come undone.

## Finishing

1 Add a shorter purple border to each side of the quilt top. Add the remaining borders to the top and bottom.

2 In the same way, add the yellow outer border.

3 Make up the quilt sandwich following the instructions on page 132.

4 Quilt in-the-ditch between each block, around the purple border. Machine-quilt a wavy line using variegated thread around the yellow border.

5 Bind the quilt and miter each corner as you come to it.

*Below: Detail showing machine quilting in the border.*

# Traditional Quilts

Simple geometric shapes, made by folding squares of paper, formed the design origins of the pieced patchwork block. Conveniently sized to make up in multiple units which, when enough blocks were completed, were assembled into a quilt top. As the traditions were established, more sophisticated ways of designing were employed, creating ever more complicated patterns, some introducing curved seams and elements of appliqué.

Many of these traditional blocks have names that relate to the environment or reflect the pastimes and people who were involved in their creation. The same block pattern is often known by different names, depending on the state in which it is made. Parallels can also be drawn between patchwork block designs and other decorative arts; similar patterns are used in tile work, for example.

The quilts in this chapter cover a range of traditional designs. In Irish Chain, two simple blocks work together to make a strong graphic statement. The Sampler Quilt is made up from four different blocks, each requiring varying skill levels. The 1930s-style Rosebud quilt is made of soft floral motifs, while the use of hand-dyed fabrics in the Eight-point Star lends a contemporary flavor.

# Broken Dishes

There is something rather appealing about anything made on a small scale. Try this quilt using blocks just 2in/5cm square. The arrangement of alternating patchwork and plain blocks belies the simplicity of the design.

Finished size: 15 x 15in/38 x 38cm
Number of blocks: 36
Finished block: 2 x 2in/5 x 5cm
Skill level: Intermediate

## Materials

◆ Navy blue print: ¼yd/0.25m
◆ Cream print: ¾yd/0.75m
◆ Navy for binding: 8 x 16in/ 20 x 41cm
◆ Low-loft batting: ½yd/0.5m square
◆ Backing: ½yd/0.5m square

## Cutting

Accurate cutting and piecing are essential when working with small blocks.

1 From the navy blue print, cut one piece 18 x 10in/ 45.75 x 25.5cm. Cut four squares each 1½in/3.75cm for the corner posts.

2 From the cream print, cut one piece 18 x 10in/ 45.75 x 25.5cm. Cut 16 squares 2½in/6.5cm. For the border, cut eight strips 6 x 1½in/ 15.25 x 3.75cm.

3 For the binding, cut four strips 1 x 16in/2.5 x 40.5cm.

## Making the Blocks

When piecing the blocks, use a ¼in/0.75cm seam. Pin and baste each stage before stitching to ensure greater accuracy.

1 To speed-piece half-square triangles, pin the cream and navy 18 x 10in/45.75 x 25.5cm pieces right sides together. Align raw edges. Press to make the fabrics "cling" together.

2 Place the cream fabric on top and use a fabric marker to accurately draw a grid of 45 squares, each 1⅞in/4.75cm.

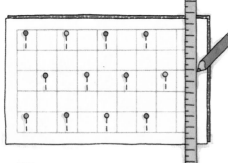

3 Draw diagonal lines through the bottom left and top right corners of each square.

4 Baste, then machine-stitch ¼in/0.75cm to each side of the drawn diagonal lines. Cut along each grid line and each diagonal line to yield 90 squares made up of two different colored triangles. Unpick the diagonal stitching at the corners, then press the seams outwards on each square.

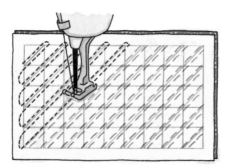

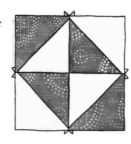

5 Arrange four squares so that each triangle sits next to a different color. Stitch the squares together to make one block. Make another 19 blocks.

6 Sew the pieced and plain blocks together into six horizontal rows, each made up of six blocks. Use the photograph as a guide.

**Border**

1 Stitch together two half-square triangles so that two navy blue triangles meet. Make up a further three rectangular blocks in the same way. (*See pic at top of next column.*)

2 Stitch each pieced rectangle between two border strips. Trim the borders to measure 13in/33cm.

3 For the left- and right-hand borders, center each pieced strip on the quilt top, aligning the navy blue triangles. With right sides together, stitch each in position.

4 For the top and bottom border, stitch a navy 1½in/3.75cm corner post to each end of the two remaining borders. Stitch the top and bottom borders in position.

5 Spread out the backing right side down on a flat surface. Smooth out any wrinkles. On top

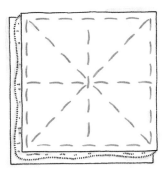

place the batting, then the quilt top right side up. Baste the layers together using long stitches.

6 Hand- or machine-quilt the surface, tracing the outline of the patchwork.

7 To bind the quilt, follow the instructions on page 133 for separate binding.

*Above: Detail of the central eight-point star motif made up of half-square triangles.*

# Eight-point Star

Hand-dyed fabrics in cool colors teamed with black
are used to make this small wallhanging. The blocks are
speed-pieced using the same technique as for Flying Geese
—a method developed by Pauline Adams.

Finished size: 16½ x 16½in/42 x 42cm
Number of blocks: 9
Finished block: 4 x 4in/10 x 10cm
Skill level: Advanced

## Materials

- Black cotton: ½yd/0.5m
- Hand-dyed cotton: ¼yd/0.25m
  in total
- Backing: ½yd/0.5m square
- Low-loft batting: ½yd/0.5m
  square

## Cutting

1 For each block, from black,
cut four corner posts 1½in/
3.75cm (36 in total). Cut nine
squares each 3¼in/8.25cm. Cut
the binding last.

2 From black, for the sashing,
cut 18 strips 1½ x 4½in/
3.75 x 11.5cm.

3 From hand-dyed fabric, cut
36 squares, 1⅞in/4.75cm.
Cut nine squares, 2½in/6.5cm.
Cut 16 corner posts 1½in/3.75cm
square for the sashing between
the eight-point star blocks.

## Making the Blocks

The star points of the block are
made using the speed-piecing
method below.

1 On the wrong side of each
1⅞in/4.75cm colored
square, draw a diagonal line
joining opposite corners.

2 Clip off the two opposite
corners at the seam
allowance as
shown.

3 On top of the right side of the larger black square, place two small, colored squares, diagonal line side up. Make sure the clipped edges meet at the center and the straight edges align with those of the black square. Pin.

4 Stitch ¼in/0.75cm to each side of the diagonal line. Cut in half along the diagonal line.

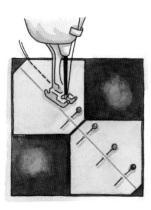

5 Press the small triangles open.

6 Add a third and fourth colored square to the remaining corners, diagonal line up. Stitch ¼in/0.75cm to each side of the line. Cut in half along the diagonal line. Press open.

7 Trim the remaining seam allowances that extend beyond the edges.

8 Arrange the remaining units and star points into a star block. Stitch the three left-hand side units together first, then the middle, then the right-hand units.

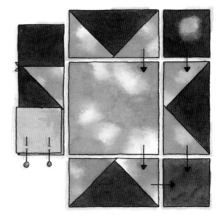

9 Stitch the three units together. Make another eight blocks in the same way.

10 Arrange the blocks into three vertical rows of three.

11 To the top of each block stitch a sashing strip. Stitch the units together into vertical rows. Stitch a sashing strip to the bottom of each block on the third row.

12 Make up four lengths of three sashing strips and four corner posts, alternating the units to begin and end with a corner post.

13 Stitch the vertical lengths between the star block rows (*right*).

14 Make up the quilt following the instructions on page 132.

15 Baste a vertical and horizontal grid through all layers with the lines of stitching

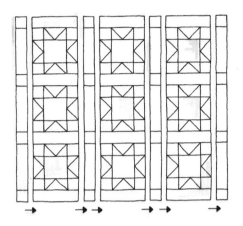

4in/10 cm apart. Baste around the outer edges.

16 Quilt in-the-ditch around the blocks and close to the seams inside each star.

17 Add the binding following the instructions on page 133 for separate binding.

# Flower Baskets

Give a contemporary look to a traditional design
with bright and bold, solid "sherbert" colors.
Also known as Goose Track and Katie's Favorite,
the complex piecing of this design makes this quilt
a challenge to the experienced stitcher.

Finished size: 20 x 20in/51 x 51cm
Number of blocks: 16
Finished block: 3½ x 3½in/9 x 9cm
Skill level: Advanced

## Materials

- Blue: ½yd/0.5m square
- Red: ½yd/0.5m square
- Apricot: ½yd/0.5m square
- Orange: ½yd/0.5m square
- Tangerine: ½yd/0.5m square
- Green: ¼yd/0.25m
- Mauve: ¼yd/0.25m
- Pink: ¼yd/0.25m
- Backing: 22in/56cm square
- Batting: 22in/56cm square
- Invisible quilting thread

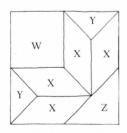

- For templates see page 136

## Cutting

1 Cut 16 squares using template W: eight from blue, two from pink, three from green, two from tangerine, and one from apricot.

2 Cut 64 shapes using template X: ten from tangerine, twelve from apricot, ten from orange, ten from red, ten from pink, and twelve from lilac.

3 Cut 32 triangles using template Y: 16 from blue, four from pink, six from green, four from tangerine, and two from apricot.

4 Cut 16 triangles from green using template Z.

5 From mauve, for the inner border, cut two strips 1½ x 16in/3.75 x 40.75cm for the quilt top and bottom, and two strips 1½ x 19in/3.75 x 48.25cm for the sides.

6 From green, for the outer border, cut two strips 1 x 19in/2.5 x 48.25cm for the top and bottom, and two 1 x 21in/2.5 x 53.5cm for the sides.

7 From pink, for the binding, cut and piece a length 2½ x 83in/6.5 x 211cm.

## Making the Blocks

Use the key (*right*) as a guide to color placement. When stitching the blocks, where seams join at an angle, begin and end stitching ¼in/0.75cm from the raw edge of the fabric.

A = Blue      E = Tangerine
B = Red      F = Green
C = Apricot      G = Mauve
D = Orange      H = Pink

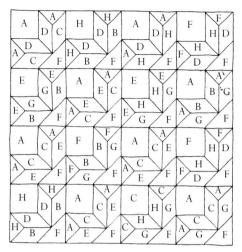

1 Each of the 16 blocks requires one square and two small triangles of the same color; four parallelograms, two each of two colors; and one large green triangle.

2 To the right-hand side of the square stitch a parallelogram.

3 Stitch a small triangle to the top right of the parallelogram. Stitch a second parallelogram to the right of the first, and to the right of the small triangle.

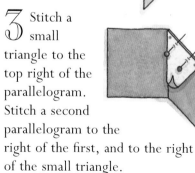

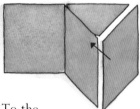

4 To the bottom of the square add a parallelogram, then a triangle and a second parallelogram.

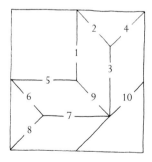

5 Add a large green triangle across the diagonal edge. Use the seam-sewing sequence above.

## Making the Quilt Top

1 Arrange the 16 blocks into the quilt top, four blocks wide and four deep. Sew the blocks into horizontal rows. Sew the rows together.

2 Add the mauve border to the top and bottom, then to each side of the quilt. Stitch the green outer border to the quilt top in the same way.

3 Make up the quilt sandwich. Baste a horizontal and vertical grid 4in/10cm apart across the surface of the quilt. Baste around the outer edges.

4 Using invisible thread, machine quilt in-the-ditch around the blocks and flower.

5 Contour-quilt ⅛in/0.5cm inside the parallelogram flower and then diagonally across the block grid to pass through the center of each flower.

6 Quilt in-the-ditch around the outer border seam and ⅛in/ 0.5cm from the seam line on the green border.

7 Bind the quilt and miter the corners as you work.

# Irish Chain

While appearing complex, this Irish Chain quilt is made up of just two blocks—checkered and plain—allowing for an ordered visual structure. Bright primary colored blocks are alternated to produce a chain effect. Accurate piecing is essential or the optical effect will be lost. The plain blocks provide space in which add quilting patterns, which enhance the visual interest of this quilt.

Finished size: 20 x 20in/51 x 51cm
Number of blocks: 9
Finished block: 5 x 5in/12.75 x 12.75cm
Skill level: Intermediate

## Materials

- Blue cotton: ¼yd/0.25m
- Red cotton: ½yd/0.5m
- Yellow print: ½yd/0.5m
- Backing: 22in/56cm square
- Compact batting: 22in/56cm square

## Cutting

1 From yellow print fabric, cut 80 squares 1½in/3.75cm—60 for the checkered blocks, 16 for the plain blocks, and four for the inner border. Cut two borders, 1¾ x 17½in/4.5 x 44.5cm, and two borders 1¾ x 21½in/4.5 x 54.5cm.

2 From red, for the checkered blocks, cut 45 squares, each 1½in/3.75cm. For the borders, cut eight strips 1½ x 7½in/3.75 x 19cm. Cut and piece a length of continuous binding 2½ x 82in/6.5 x 208cm.

3 From blue, cut 24 squares each 1½in/3.75cm—20 for the checkered blocks and four for the inner border. Cut eight rectangles 1½ x 3½in/3.75 x 9cm for the plain blocks, and four rectangles 3½ x 5½in/9 x 14cm for the plain block centers.

## Making the Checkered Blocks

1 For the five checkered blocks, you will need nine red, four blue, and twelve yellow print squares.

2 Arrange the 25 squares using the illustrations below.

3 Stitch the squares into rows using ¼in/0.75cm seams.

4 Stitch the rows together into a block.

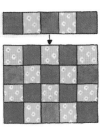

## Making the Plain Blocks

1 For each of the four plain blocks, you will need one large blue rectangle, two small rectangles, and four yellow print squares. Arrange the units into the block pattern.

2 Stitch the units into rows. Stitch the rows together.

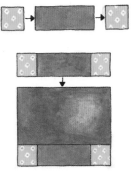

3 Arrange the blocks using the picture below as a guide.

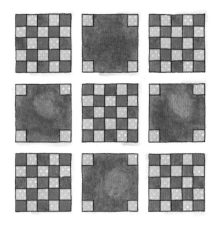

4 Stitch the blocks into horizontal rows. Stitch the rows together.

## Borders

1 For the inner border, sew a red strip to two sides of each blue square. Make four. Stitch two borders to opposite sides of the quilt.

2 Stitch a yellow square to each end of the two remaining borders. Stitch the borders to the quilt.

3 For the outer border, add a shorter yellow border to two sides of the quilt. Stitch the longer yellow borders to the top and bottom.

## Finishing

1 Make up the quilt sandwich following the instructions on page 132. Baste a grid 4in/10cm apart through all layers.

2 On the plain blocks, draw diagonal lines across the block surface.

3 Machine-quilt diagonal lines across the quilt surface. Quilt the center of the inner border. Quilt three straight lines around the outer border. Trim the quilt to measure 20in/51cm square.

4 Bind the quilt with double fold binding and miter the corners (*see page 133*).

# Rosebud Garden

Representational patchwork works best when the lines are kept straight and the shapes simple. The center diamond—a nine-patch block set on-point—effectively offsets the stylized blocks of the rosebuds.

Finished size: 22 x 22in/56 x 56cm
Number of blocks: 8
Finished block: 4 x 4in/10 x 10cm
Skill level: Confident intermediate

## Materials

- Pink print for the rosebuds and center block: ¼yd/0.25m
- Green print for the rosebud blocks: ¼yd/0.25m
- Cream solid for the rosebud blocks: ¼yd/0.25m
- Cream print for the center block: ¼yd/0.25m
- Blue print: ¾yd/0.75m
- Backing: 24in/61cm square
- Batting: 24in/61cm square

## Cutting

1 From pink print, for the rosebuds, cut eight squares 2in/5cm. For the quilt center, cut one square 4in/10cm.

2 From green print, for the foliage around the rosebud, cut eight rectangles 2 x 1¼in/5 x 3.25cm. Cut eight rectangles 2¾ x 1¼in/7 x 3.25cm. For the leaves, cut 16 squares 2in/5cm. For the stems, cut eight strips 3 x ¾in/ 7.5 x 2cm.

3 From solid cream, for the leaves, cut 16 rectangles 2¾ x 2in/7 x 5cm. For the areas around the stems, cut eight squares 2½in/6.5cm. For the diamond border, cut two strips 1 x 12in/2.5 x 30.5cm and two strips 1 x 13in/2.5 x 33cm.

4 From cream print, for the center panel, cut four squares 4in/10cm.

5 From blue print, cut four squares 5½in/14cm. Cut each in half across one diagonal to yield eight triangles. Cut four outer borders, 24 x 2½in/61 x 6.5cm.

6 For the double-fold binding, cut and piece a length of blue print 2½ x 90in/6.5 x 229cm.

## Leaves

1 To make the leaves, on the wrong side of each 2in/5cm green square, draw a diagonal line joining two corners.

2 Place a green square on a solid cream rectangle, right sides together and aligning short raw edges.

3 Stitch on the line, reinforcing the stitching at each end.

4 Trim away below the stitching line and press the piece out flat. Make two for each rosebud block.

## Stems

1 Cut each cream 2½in/6.5cm square in half across the diagonal to yield 16 triangles.

2 With right sides together, align the long edge of the stem with the diagonal raw edge of the cream triangle. Stitch the two together and press open.

3 Stitch another cream triangle to the other side of the stem and press the seams to one side.

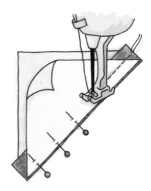

4 Trim the unit to 2in/5cm square, ensuring the stem is in the center.

## Buds

1 Stitch one green foliage 2 x 1¼in/5 x 3cm rectangle to one side of the pink rosebud square. Press.

2 Stitch the second 2¾ x 1¼in/7 x 3cm rectangle to an adjacent side.

3 Stitch one leaf unit to the base of the rosebud unit.

4 Stitch the remaining leaf unit to the stem unit.

5 Stitch the two pieces together. Make eight blocks and trim to 4in/10cm square.

## Assembling the Quilt Top

1 Following the photograph, arrange the units for the center nine-patch diamond on a clean, flat surface.

2 Stitch the blocks into three rows of three. Stitch the rows together, aligning all seams.

3 To two opposite sides of the nine-patch, with right sides together, stitch a shorter cream solid border. Trim the short ends even with the quilt top.

4 Stitch a cream border to the top and bottom of the quilt center. Trim the ends.

5 To make the corners, make sure the orientation of each rosebud block matches the photograph. Align the bottom edge of each rosebud block with the 5½in/14cm edge of one blue triangle. Align the right-hand straight edges. Pin and stitch in place. Press.

6 Align a second blue triangle with the adjacent side of the rosebud block, aligning right-

hand straight edges and pinning the triangle across the tip of the first blue triangle. Stitch. Make four corners.

7 Stitch a corner to opposite sides of the nine-patch, then to the remaining sides. Press.

8 Stitch a border to each side of the quilt top, mitering each corner as you work. Follow the instructions on page 131.

*Above: Detail of rosebud motif.*

9 Make up the quilt sandwich and baste a grid of 4in/10cm squares across the quilt top. Baste around the outer edges.

10 Machine-quilt close to the seams and around the edges of the inner squares and outer triangles. Machine-quilt the solid cream areas of the rosebud blocks and ¼in/0.75cm from the seams. Quilt close to the seams along the borders.

11 Bind the quilt to finish, following the instructions on page 133.

# Bear's Paw

This block pattern, which utilizes half-square triangles, is known by various names—Hand of Friendship, Duck's Foot in the Mud, and Bear's Paw. In this crib quilt, the blocks are set on-point and made in alternating color schemes.

Finished size: 41 x 31in/104.25 x 78.75cm
Number of blocks: 8
Finished block: 7 x 7in/17.75 x 17.75cm
Skill level: Advanced

## Materials

- Pink print: ¾yd/0.75m
- Blue print: ¾yd/0.75m
- Pink solid: 1yd/1m
- Blue solid: ¾yd/0.75m
- Backing: 43 x 33in/110 x 84cm
- Batting: 43 x 33in/110 x 84cm

## Cutting

**1** From the pink print, for the half-square triangles, cut six pieces 9 x 5in/23 x 12.75cm. Cut eight squares 2½in/6.5cm. Cut six squares 1½in/3.75cm for the block centers. Cut the borders last.

**2** From the blue print, for the half-square triangles, cut two pieces 9 x 5in/23 x 12.75cm. Cut 24 squares each 2½in/6.5cm for the bear's paw. Cut two squares 1½in/3.75cm for the center post of four blocks. Cut 24 sashing strips 7½ x 1½in/19 x 3.75cm. Cut four squares 3½in/9cm for the border.

**3** From pink, for the half-square triangles, cut two pieces 9 x 5in/23 x 12.75cm. Cut eight squares 1½in/3.75cm for the corners of the bear's paw. Cut eight rectangles 3½ x 1½in/ 9 x 3.75cm. Cut 17 corner posts 1½in/3.75cm.

**4** From pink, for the side triangles, cut one square 12¾in/32.5cm. Cut across both diagonals to yield four triangles. Make a template from one triangle and cut two more—six in total.

**5** From pink, for the corner triangles, cut two squares 7¼in/18.5cm. Cut each in half across one diagonal.

6 From pink, for the binding, cut two strips 42 x 2½in/ 106.75 x 6.5cm, and two strips 32 x 2½in/81.25 x 6.5cm.

7 From blue, for the half-square triangles, cut six pieces 9 x 5in/23 x 12.75cm. Cut 24 squares 1½in/3.75cm for the corners of the bear's paw. Cut 24 rectangles 3½ x 1½in/9 x 3.75cm.

## Making Half-square Triangles

1 With right sides together, pair up each pink print 9 x 5in/23 x 12.75cm rectangle with a same size solid blue. Repeat with the blue print and solid pink rectangles. Press.

2 On the wrong side of the lighter fabric, draw a rectangle 7½ x 3¾in/19 x 9.5cm.

3 Inside, draw a grid of eight squares 1⅞in/4.75cm—four across and two down.

4 Draw diagonal lines, in one direction only, joining the corners of the squares.

*Right: Detail of one bear's paw.*

5 Stitch ¼in/0.75cm to each side of the diagonal lines.

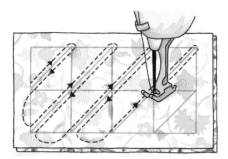

6 Cut along the drawn vertical and horizontal grid and along the diagonal lines. Unpick the few stitches that cross some of the corners. Press the seams toward the darkest fabric. Each set of rectangles makes 16 half-square triangles—enough for one block.

7 To make one bear's paw, stitch together two half-square triangle units, ensuring the solids and prints face the same direction. Stitch together two units, reversing the orientation (*see below for a color guide*).

8 Stitch one print 2½in/6.5cm square to the left of two half-square triangle units.

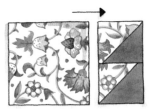

9 Stitch a 1½in/3.75cm square to the right of two half-square triangles.

10 Stitch the units together. Repeat.

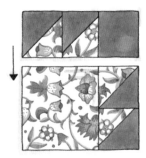

11 To make one block, stitch a 3½ x 1½in/9 x 3.75cm unit between two bear's paws, ensuring that the paws are facing in the correct direction. Repeat.

12 Stitch a 1½in/3.75cm square between two 3½ x 1½in/9 x 3.75cm units. Stitch this strip between the two blocks.

## Assembling the Quilt Top

1 Refer to the quilt assembly diagram (*fig 1, top right*).

2 Stitch the vertical sashing to the blocks and join the required number together for each row, ensuring the correct color sequence.

3 For the horizontal sashing with corner posts, stitch together the units for each row.

4 Arrange the units into the quilt top as shown in the diagram (*fig 2. below right*). Note that the side and two corner triangles are added as the quilt top is constructed.

5 Stitch sashing to the top and bottom two rows. Leave the long center sashing until last. Add the appropriate side or corner triangle.

6 Add the two remaining corner triangles.

7 Stitch the shorter borders to the top and bottom of the quilt top.

8 To each end of the remaining borders, stitch a corner post. Then stitch the borders to each side of the quilt top.

9 Make up the quilt sandwich and baste a vertical and horizontal grid.

10 Quilt around the bear's paw motifs close to the seams and along the sashing strips. Quilt the side and corner triangles in lines parallel to the sides of the blocks and 1in/2.5cm apart. Quilt around the border close to the seam.

11 Bind the quilt to finish (*see page 133*).

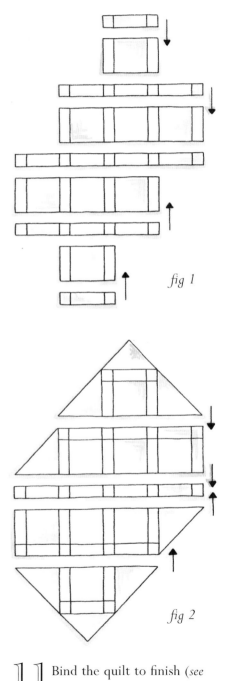

*fig 1*

*fig 2*

# Sampler Quilt

Blue and pink plaid and striped shirting material are used to effect in this small sampler quilt. Four blocks of varying complexity will introduce a beginner to new piecing skills.

Finished size: 27 x 27in/68.5 x 68.5cm
Finished block: 9in/23cm
Skill level: Confident beginner/intermediate

## Materials

♦ Eleven fabrics in a variety of pink and blue plaids and stripes: ⅛yd/10cm of each.
♦ Pink for sashing: ½yd/0.5m
♦ Blue for the border: ½yd/0.5m
♦ Plaid for the binding: ½yd/0.5m
♦ Backing: 29in/74cm square
♦ Batting: 29in/74cm square

♦ For templates see page 138

*Opposite:*
Nine-patch (*top left*)
Churn Dash (*top right*)
Mother's Delight (*bottom left*)
Card Trick (*bottom right*)

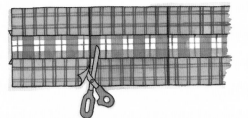

## Cutting and Making the Nine-patch Block

The nine-patch block is made up of three units—a center square, a nine-patch, and a pieced square.

1 For the center block, cut one blue check square 3½in/9cm.

2 For the pieced squares, cut two pink strips 1½ x 15in/ 3.75 x 38cm. Cut one blue strip the same size.

3 Join the three strips together with the blue in the middle. Cross-cut the strip into four segments, each 3½in/9cm long.

4 For column A of the small nine-patch (*see column 1 page 78*), cut two blue and one pink strip 1½ x 15in/3.75 x 38cm.

5 Join as before with the pink unit in the center. Cross-cut into eight segments each 1½in/ 3.75cm wide.

6 For column B of the small nine-patch, cut two pink and one blue strip 1½ x 8in/3.75 x 20.25cm.

7 Join as before, alternating the colors, and cross-cut into four segments each 1½in/ 3.75cm.

8 Sew four nine-patch squares following the configuration on page 78.

A     B     A

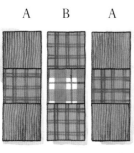

*Fig 1*

9 Arrange the nine units. Stitch into horizontal rows, then stitch the rows together.

## Cutting and Making the Mother's Delight Block

The mother's delight block is assembled first into eighths and then into quarters.

1 Make templates from the patterns provided.

2 Using template 1, cut four dark blue triangles (A). Reverse the template and cut four mid-blue triangles (B), for the inside star.

3 Using template 2, cut four pink triangles (C). Reverse the template and cut four blue triangles (D). Cut four pink stripe triangles for the outer edges. Reverse the unit and cut four more (E).

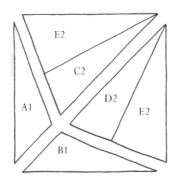

4 Stitch units C and E, and D and E together. Add unit A to the base of C/E, and B to the base of D/E.

5 Stitch the two units together, then press the seam open.

6 Stitch four quarters to make the block.

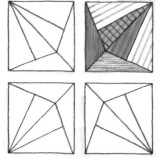

## Cutting and Making the Churn Dash Block

The block (*top left in photograph*) is made up of one center square (A), four pieced squares (B), and four half-square triangles (C).

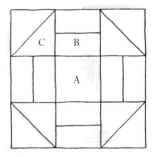

1 For A, cut one square 3½in/ 9cm.

2 For B, cut one blue and one pink strip 2 x 15in/5 x 38cm.

3 Stitch together along the long edge. Cross-cut into four segments 3½in/9cm long.

4 For C, cut two pink and two blue squares each 3⅞in/ 9.75cm. Follow the instructions on page 14, steps 1–4, to make four half-square triangles.

5 Arrange units A, B, and C into the block. Stitch into rows. Stitch the rows together.

## Cutting and Making the Card Trick Block

The Card Trick block (*bottom right*) is made up of three units—half-square triangles for each corner (A), quarter square triangles for the center (C), and one large triangle with two small triangles (B).

1 Make templates from the patterns provided.

2 Cut two large and two small triangles from each of four shades of blue.

3 Cut four large and four small triangles from pink.

4 Arrange the units using the photograph on page 76 as a guide to color and placement.

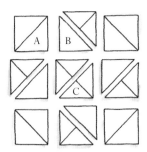

5 Stitch together the large triangles that make up the corner units (*see page 14*).

6 For the center, stitch two pairs of triangles together. Stitch the units together.

7 For the remaining blocks, stitch together the smaller triangles into pairs. Stitch this unit to the large triangle.

8 Stitch the blocks into vertical rows. Stitch the three rows together, aligning seams.

## Assembling the Quilt

1 From pink, for the sashing, cut strips 1½in/3.75cm wide in the following lengths: two 9½in/24cm lengths, three 19½in/49.5cm lengths, and two 21½in/54.5cm lengths.

2 Stitch one short sashing strip between each of two blocks. Stitch a 19½in/49.5cm length between the two halves of the quilt top and to the quilt top and bottom. Stitch the two remaining lengths to each side.

3 Cut four borders 3 x 29in/ 7.5 x 73.75cm. Stitch each in place, mitering the corners.

4 Make up the quilt sandwich. Baste a horizontal and vertical grid across the quilt surface.

5 Quilt in-the-ditch along the seam lines of the sashing, border, Churn Dash, Card Trick, and Nine-patch blocks.

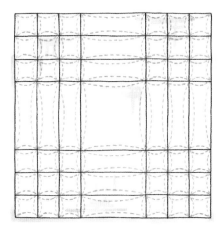

6 Contour quilt ¼in/0.75cm from the seam lines on all the patches of the Churn Dash block. Free-motion quilt the background of the Card Trick block or use hand running stitch.

7 Cut and piece a length of continuous binding 2½ x 116in/6.5 x 295cm. Bind to finish and miter the corners.

# Appliqué

Appliqué, the art of stitching one fabric to another for decorative effect, is one of the oldest forms of needlework. Appliqué quilts range in style from examples of "folk art," such as the Christmas Quilt, to sophisticated masterpieces, such as the mid-nineteenth-century "Baltimore" quilts made by skilled needlewomen, as well as the intricate reverse appliqué style of Mola work.

Appliqué lends itself to pictorial interpretations and will appeal to quilters who enjoy "building" pictures rather than piecing a quilt.

A variety of appliqué styles and methods are represented. Two of the most popular are: fusible webbing, a modern, labor-saving invention where one layer of fabric is adhered to another using the heat of an iron; and freezer appliqué, ideal for those who prefer hand work.

Patchwork can be successfully combined with appliqué; for example, Autumn Leaves uses speed-piecing techniques with a traditional block design, the Mola quilt is worked in blocks and stitched together at the end, and the Christmas Quilt has hand-appliquéd motifs over a simple pieced background.

# Autumn Leaves

Appliqué leaves drift downward against a patchwork of traditional maple leaf blocks. The techniques used combine speed-piecing and machine appliqué using fusible webbing.

Finished size: 21 x 21in/53.5 x 53.5cm
Number of blocks: 4
Finished block: 6 x 6in/15.25 x 15.25cm
Skill level: Enthusiastic intermediate

## Materials

- Three fabrics with leaf print designs:
  A and B: ½yd/0.5m of each
  C: ¼yd/0.25m square
- Four different leaf-print fabrics for the background blocks:
  6in/15.25cm square
- Scraps of large motif prints for the leaves
- Scraps of fusible webbing
- Scraps of tearaway stabilizer
- Backing: 23 x 23in/59 x 59cm
- Batting: 23 x 23in/59 x 59cm
- Variegated machine embroidery thread

- For templates see page 138

## Cutting

**1** From fabric A, for the maple leaf blocks, cut one piece 14 x 8in/35.5 x 20.25cm. For the sawtooth border, cut one piece 15 x 12in/38 x 30.5cm.

**2** Cut the same from fabric B.

**3** For the maple leaf blocks, from the 6in/15cm squares, cut three 4½in/11.5cm squares. From C, cut four squares each 2½in/6.5cm. From a remnant of A or B, cut one square 4½in/ 11.5cm .

**4** From fabric C, for the corner triangles, cut two squares 9½in/24.25cm. Cut each in half across the diagonal.

**5** For the border corner posts, cut four squares 2⅛in/ 5.25cm from scraps.

**6** Following the instructions on page 129, make templates for each of the leaves.

**7** For the leaves, bond fusible webbing to the reverse of the fabric scraps. On the paper side of the web, draw around the leaf templates. Cut the required number.

**8** From any fabric, for the binding, cut four strips each 2½ x 22in/6.5 x 56cm.

## Making the Blocks

**1** For the half-square triangles in the four center blocks, place the 14 x 8in/35.5 x 20.25cm pieces of A and B right sides together.

**2** On the lighter fabric, draw a grid of squares, four across x two down each 2⅞in/7.25cm.

**3** Following steps 1–6 of the Bear's Paw block on page 74, make 16 bicolor half-square triangles.

**4** Arrange four half-square triangles, one 4½in/ 11.5cm square and one 2½in/6.5cm square into the block

**5** Follow steps 7–10 of the Bear's Paw quilt on page 74 to make one block. Make three more blocks.

**6** Stitch the four blocks together into a square.

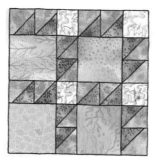

**7** Stitch a corner triangle to each side of the center block.

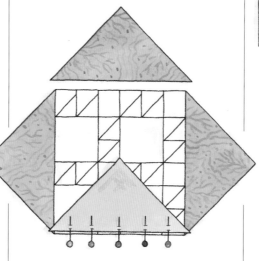

## Sawtooth Border

**1** Place the 15 x 12in/38 x 30.5cm fabrics A and B right sides together. On the wrong side of the lighter fabric, accurately draw a grid of twenty squares 2½in/6.5cm—five across and four down.

**2** Repeat steps 3–6 of the Bear's Paw quilt as before to make 40 bicolor squares.

**3** For each border, stitch five squares together, ensuring the orientation of each print is in the same direction. Then stitch five squares together, reversing the orientation.

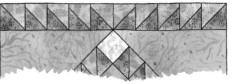

**4** Stitch the two halves of the border together, adjusting the center squares to make the border fit the quilt top.

**5** Make three more borders in the same way.

**6** Stitch a border to the top and bottom of the quilt.

**7** Stitch a 2⅛in/5.25cm corner post to each end of two remaining borders.

**8** Stitch the borders to each side of the quilt top.

*Opposite: Close-up detail of leaves.*

## Appliqué

1 To add the leaves, remove the paper backing from the fusible webbing. Place each leaf as desired on the right side of the quilt. Fuse in place following the manufacturer's instructions.

2 To prevent the work from puckering while stitching, place tearaway stabilizer behind the quilt top. Using machine embroidery thread, satin stitch around the outline of the leaves. Tear away the stabilizer.

## Finishing

1 Make up the quilt sandwich, following the instructions on page 132. Baste a 4in/10cm grid on the quilt surface and around the edges.

2 Avoiding the border and the appliqué leaves, free-motion quilt the surface of the patchwork (*see page 132*). Quilt in-the-ditch between the seams joining the sawtooth border. Bind the quilt to finish (*see page 133*).

# Folk Art Meets Jazz

The technique of reverse appliqué involves cutting away layers of fabric to reveal the design. This is an improvisational piece: you can create any block design you choose.

Finished size: 20 x 20in/51 x 51cm
Number of blocks: 16
Finished block: 4½ x 4½in/11.5 x11.5cm
Skill level: Confident beginner

## Materials

- Selection of bright solid colors for the quilt top at least 5in/12.75cm square
- Black: ¼yd/0.25m
- Turquoise: ¼yd/0.25m
- Backing: 22in/56cm square
- Batting: 22in/56cm square
- Tearaway stabilizer: 1yd/1m
- Scraps of fusible webbing
- Selection of hand and machine embroidery threads
- Invisible machine quilting thread
- Thin cardboard

- For templates see page 139

## Cutting

1 From the selection of solid colors, cut 32 squares each 5in/12.75cm

2 Cut 16 squares of tearaway stabilizer at least 5in/12.75cm.

3 From black, for the border, cut strips 2½in/6.5cm wide across the width of the fabric.

4 To make templates of the heart, star, and circle, trace the patterns provided. Cut out the shapes and stick to thin cardboard. The fabric shapes are cut at a later stage.

5 From turquoise, for the binding, cut strips 2½in/6.5cm wide across the width of the fabric.

## Making the Appliqués

1 To make the reverse appliqué patches, arrange the 32 squares into pairs, choosing colors that complement or contrast with each other.

2 Place the pairs together, right sides uppermost, and steam press so that the fabrics "cling" together.

3 With a ruler and fabric marker, draw three or four straight lines and random zigzag lines across the surface of the uppermost piece.

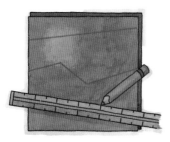

4 Machine straight stitch along the drawn lines.

5 With a pair of sharp embroidery scissors, carefully cut away the top layer of fabric in alternate areas to reveal the second fabric. Cut close to the stitching line but do not cut into

it. Put the waste fabric aside to use at step 11.

6 Place a square of tearaway stabilizer underneath the block and pin to hold.

7 Refer to your stitch manual and set the sewing machine dial to close satin stitch or buttonhole stitch.

8 Stitch along the drawn line, covering the raw edges and the machine straight stitch and removing the pins as you come to them. Tear away the stabilizer.

9 Turn the piece to the wrong side. Where a double layer

of fabric remains, cut away the second fabric, close to the machine stitching. Make 15 more blocks in the same way.

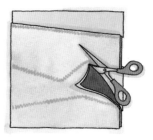

10 To add the heart, circle, and star appliqués, bond fusible webbing to the wrong side of any fabrics left over, following the manufacturer's instructions.

11 Trace the template shapes onto the paper side of the fusible webbing and cut out the required number. Remove the paper backing.

12 Place the shapes webbing side down on the blocks and fuse in place, following the manufacturer's instructions.

13 Embroider around the outline of the motifs using blanket stitch.

## Assembling the Quilt

1 Arrange the 16 blocks into the quilt top.

2 With right sides together, stitch the blocks into four rows of four. Stitch the rows together, ensuring the seams are aligned. Press.

3 Add the borders, stitching the strips to the top and bottom first and trimming away the excess fabric before stitching borders to the sides.

4 Make up the quilt sandwich and baste a grid through all layers and around the outer edges of the quilt top.

*Above: Detail of heart and star motifs.*

5 Quilt in-the-ditch along the seam lines of the blocks using invisible machine quilting thread. Using brightly colored threads, quilt in straight lines across the blocks, echoing the lines of the reverse appliqué.

6 Bind the quilt with double-fold binding (*see page 133*).

# Mola Quilt

Based on a traditional Mola quilt, layers of unusual fabrics are built up to create a rich surface of texture and metallic color. A final layer of solid color is placed on top and is cut away to reveal the fabrics beneath. The technique of cutting away from the top is similar to reverse appliqué.

Finished size: 37 x 37in/94 x 94cm

Number of blocks: 25

Finished block: 6 x 6in/15.25 x 15.25cm

Skill level: Advanced

## Materials

- White cotton for the background: 1yd/1m
- Pale yellow (A) for the first layer: ¼yd/0.25m
- Speckled yellow (B) for the first layer: ½yd/0.5m
- Mustard (C) for the first layer: ¼yd/0.25m
- Patterned yellow (D) for the first layer: ¼yd/20cm
- Black cotton for the second layer: ⅛yd/10cm
- Metallic black and gold for the third layer: 1yd/1m
- Black sheer for the fourth layer: 12in/30.5cm

- Copper lurex for the fifth layer: 10in/25cm square
- Five different shades of red for the top layer and outer border: ¼yd/0.25m of each
- Binding: ½yd/0.5m
- Yellow machine embroidery thread
- Spray glue
- Backing: 40in/102cm square
- Batting: 40in/102cm square
- Tearaway stabilizer

- For template see page 137

## Cutting

1 From white, cut 25 squares each 7in/18cm.

2 From A, cut two squares 7in/18cm. Cross-cut one square across each diagonal to yield four triangles.

3 From B, cut five squares 7in/18cm. Cross-cut one square across each diagonal to yield four triangles. Cut each remaining square into four smaller squares. Cross-cut each small square across one diagonal to yield two triangles.

4 From C, cut three squares 7in/18cm. Cut two squares in half to yield four rectangles 3½ x 7in/9 x 18cm. Cut the remaining square into four smaller squares.

5 From D, cut two squares each 7in/18cm. Cut each into four small squares. Cut each small square across one diagonal.

6 For the second layer, from black cotton, cut 25 squares each 2½in/6.5cm.

7 From metallic black, cut 25 squares 5in/12.75cm. Fray ⅛in/0.5cm of the raw edges.

8 From sheer black, cut 25 squares 3¾in/9.5cm. Fray ¼in/0.75cm around the outer edge.

9 From copper, cut 25 squares 1¾in/4.5cm.

10 Cut the red for the Mola work as you need it. For the inner and outer borders, from different shades of red, cut eight strips 2in/5cm wide x the width of the fabric.

*Right: Detail showing the layered effect of the Mola work.*

11 For the binding, cut and piece a length 2½ x 156in/6.5 x 397cm from gray.

### Assembling the Background

1 Using the plan (*right*) as a guide, position each A, B, C, and D triangle, rectangle, and square on each white background square, aligning raw edges. Spray glue each into place temporarily.

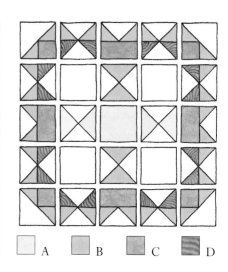

A    B    C    D

2 Using yellow thread, machine zigzag the outer edges of each shape only, beginning 2in/5cm from the outside edge.

3 In the center of each background, spray glue a black cotton square, right side up.

4 Center a metallic black and gold square on top and spray glue to hold. Place a black sheer square on top. Add a copper square to the center.

### Mola Work

The top left block represents the center square of the quilt. The quilt is symmetrical.

1 Cut squares, rectangles, and triangles of red large enough to cover each block, according to the diagram below.

2 Trace the Mola template onto tearaway stabilizer. Using the diagram as your guide, pin each to the red fabrics. Pin the red fabrics to the block surface.

3 Sew long running stitches through all the layers along the lines of the pattern. These lines of stitching anchor the red to the background and should be removed after step 5.

4 Tear away the paper. Using sharp embroidery scissors, cut the red fabric halfway between the lines of stitching. Turn in ⅛in/0.5cm of the red.

5 Hem stitch in place. The finished strips of the pattern should be ¼in/0.75cm.

### Assembling the Quilt

1 Join the blocks into rows. Join the rows together.

2 Add the inner border to the sides, top, and bottom. Trim the width of the strips to 1in/2.5cm. Add the outer border.

3 Make up the quilt sandwich. Tie quilt the layers at the intersections of all the squares using appropriate color thread.

4 Quilt the border by extending the diagonal lines formed by the Mola work into the edges of the quilt.

5 To finish, bind the quilt, then embellish the quilt top with couching and small knots of threads made into half pompoms.

# Ducklings Quilt

Brightly colored appliqué ducklings offset against plaids and checks make this design ideal for a crib quilt.

Finished size: 29½ x 36½in/75 x 92.75cm
Finished block 6 x 6in/15.25 x 15.25cm
Skill level: Intermediate

## Materials

- Blue stripe for blocks and binding: ½yd/0.5m
- Yellow solid for blocks and ducklings: ½yd/0.5m
- Blue check for ducks and wings: ½yd/0.5m
- Light blue solid for wings: ½yd/0.5m square
- Medium blue solid for center block: ½yd/0.5m square
- Dark blue scraps for wings
- Turquoise gingham: ½yd/0.5m square
- Navy gingham: ½yd/0.5m square
- Yellow plaid: ½yd/0.5m
- Fusible webbing
- Tearaway stabilizer
- Machine embroidery thread
- Embroidery thread
- Backing: 32 x 39in/82 x 99cm
- Batting: 32 x 39in/82 x 99cm

- For templates see page 139

## Cutting

1 For the background, from blue stripe, cut seven squares 6½in/16.5cm. Cut the same from yellow.

2 For the center block, from medium blue cut a rectangle 12 x 11in/30.5 x 28cm.

3 Make cardboard templates for the duck and duckling.

4 Bond and cut five right-facing and two left-facing ducklings from blue check and yellow—14 in total.

5 Bond and cut one large duck from blue check. Cut a second large duck from yellow, reversing the orientation. Use the photograph as a guide.

6 Bond and cut seven blue check wings and seven light blue wings for the ducklings.

7 Bond and cut one dark blue wing for the blue check duck and one blue check wing for the yellow duck.

8 Bond and cut 14 beaks and eyes from light blue for the ducklings and two dark blue beaks for the ducks.

9 Bond and cut two blue stripe collars.

10 From turquoise gingham cut two sashing strips, 1¼ x 12in/3 x 30.5cm, and two 1¼ x 14in/3 x 35.5cm for the sides of the center panel. Cut ten turquoise strips 1½ x 6½in/3.75 x 16.5cm for the sashing.

11 From navy gingham, cut two strips 1½ x 20½in/ 3.75 x 52cm and two strips 1½ x 27in/3.75 x 68.75cm for the border of the center medallion.

12 From yellow plaid, cut two strips 3½ x 13½in/ 9 x 34.25cm for above and below the center panel. Cut two strips 1½ x 34½in/3.75 x 87.5cm, and two strips 1½ x 25½in/3.75 x 64.75cm for the inner border of the quilt.

*Below: Detail of a duckling.*

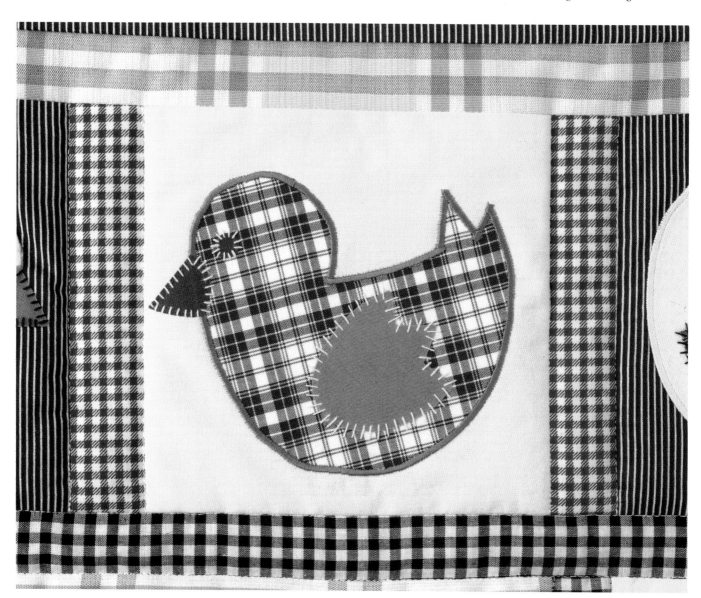

## Ducks and Ducklings

1 Center each blue check duckling on the right side of a yellow square. Remove the paper backing and fuse each in position following the manufacturer's instructions. Fuse a yellow duckling to the center of a blue check square.

2 Fuse each large duck to the medium blue center panel.

3 Place a sheet of tearaway stabilizer behind each block and machine satin stitch around the outline, over the raw edges of each duck and duckling. Tear away the stabilizer.

4 Bond each wing, beak, and eye to a duckling, using the photograph as a color guide. Embroider the outlines with a decorative straight stitch.

## Assembling the Quilt Top

1 Stitch each 12in/30.5cm turquoise sashing to the top and bottom of the medallion.

2 Stitch the longer sashing to the sides. Add the yellow plaid strips to the top and bottom of the medallion.

3 Stitch a 20½in/52cm navy gingham strip to each side of the medallion.

4 Arrange the duckling blocks around the medallion, alternating the color sequence. The center top and bottom ducklings face each other.

5 Position the 6½in/16.5cm turquoise sashing between the duckling blocks. Stitch

together four blocks and three sashing strips for the top and bottom of the quilt, and three blocks and two sashing strips for the sides.

6 Stitch the shorter duckling panels to each side of the quilt top.

7 Stitch a 27in/68.75cm navy gingham strip across the top and bottom.

8 Stitch the remaining duckling panels to the top and bottom of the quilt.

9 Stitch a yellow plaid border across the top and bottom, then the sides of the quilt.

10 Make up the quilt sandwich (see page 132). Baste a horizontal and vertical grid, avoiding stitching through the duck shapes.

11 Quilt in-the-ditch around all of the blocks. Cut binding 2½in/6.5cm wide and bind to finish (see page 133).

# Christmas Quilt

Christmas reindeer leap across a pieced patchwork
background made up of squares and rectangles.
The method is quick and easy: appliqué shapes are ironed in
place using fusible webbing.
The folk art quality of the design lends itself to the use
of homespun plaids and hand-dyed cottons.

Finished size: 24 x 24in/61 x 61cm
Skill level: Intermediate

## Materials

Selection of plaid, patterned,
and hand-dyed large fabric scraps
in the following colors and
quantities:
◆ Green for the border and trees:
36 x 9in/91.5 x 23cm in total
◆ Red for the border and
reindeer: ½yd/0.5m square
in total
◆ Yellow for the border, moon,
and stars: large scraps
◆ Blue for the quilt center:
½yd/0.5m square in total,
the largest scrap to measure
18 x 8½in/45.75 x 21.5cm

◆ Red and green stranded cotton
in a variety of shades for the
blanket stitch decoration
◆ Chalk marker for quilting
◆ An assortment of decorative
wooden buttons
◆ Beads for the eyes
◆ Backing: 26in/66cm square
◆ Batting: 26in/66cm square
◆ Thin cardboard

◆ For templates see page 140

## Cutting

1 Make a template for each of
the appliqué shapes.

2 On the paper side of fusible
webbing, using the templates
as a guide, draw two large and
three small trees, with a
½in/1.5cm gap between each.
Draw three large stars, a moon,
and two reindeer. Cut out each
shape, ¼in/0.75cm larger all
around than the drawn shape.

3 Bond each shape to the
wrong side of an appro-
priately colored fabric scrap.
Cut out each on the drawn line.
Do not remove the backing.

4 Referring to the quilt plan (*right*) cut the following:

**Blue**

A = 17½ x 4½in/44.5 x 11.5cm
B = 11½ x 6½in/29 x 16.5cm
C = 6½ x 6½in/16.5 x 16.5cm
D = 17½ x 7½in/44.5 x 19cm

**Green**

E = 10¼ x 3½in/26 x 9cm
F = 10¼ x 3½in/26 x 9cm
G = 3½ x 3½in/9 x 9cm
H = 4½ x 3½in/11.5 x 9cm

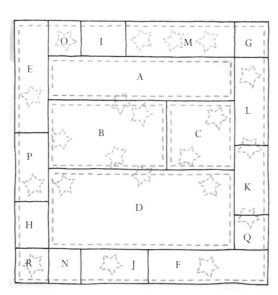

I = 4½ x 3½in/11.5 x 9cm
J = 6½ x 3½in/16.5 x 9cm
K = 6½ x 3½in/16.5 x 9cm
L = 8½ x 3½in/21.5 x 9cm

**Red**

M = 10¼ x 3½in/26 x 9cm
N = 3½ x 3½in/9 x 9cm
O = 3½ x 3½in/9 x 9cm
P = 6½ x 3½in/16.5 x 9cm

**Yellow**

Q = 3½ x 3½in/9 x 9cm
R = 4½ x 3½in/11.5 x 9cm

*Above: Detail of appliqué moon and star motifs, showing the blanket stitch around the edges.*

## Assembling the Background

1 For the pieced background, stitch B to C. Stitch A to the top of this unit, then stitch D to the bottom of the unit.

2 Using a ¼in/0.75cm seam, stitch together O, I, and M to form the top border.

3 Stitch together the left-hand border—E, P, and H.

4 Stitch together the right-hand border—G, L, K, and Q.

5 Stitch together the bottom border—R, N, J, and F.

6 Stitch the top border to the quilt center. Add the left- and right-hand borders to each side, then add the bottom border. Press carefully.

## Appliqués

1 Arrange each appliqué shape on the background, right side up. Remove the paper backing and fuse each in place. Fuse those that are overlapped first.

2 Blanket stitch around the outer edge of each motif using two strands of contrasting embroidery thread.

## Finishing

1 Make up the quilt sandwich (*see page 132*).

2 Make a cardboard template of the small star. Place the template on the quilt surface in the required positions and draw around it with a chalk marker. Refer to the layout.

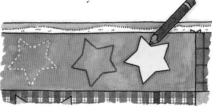

3 Handquilt stars and straight lines using the quilt plan as your guide.

4 Baste around the raw edge of the quilt top. To self-bind the quilt, cut the batting to the same size as the quilt top. Turn in the corners of the backing and trim away leaving a small seam allowance. Turn under a small seam around the raw edge of the backing. Bring the folded edge over the raw edges of the quilt front. Pin. Slipstitch in place.

5 Sew on beads for the reindeers' eyes. Then add wooden buttons as desired.

# Rabbit Patch

This charming wallhanging, with its stylized floral motifs, twisted vines, and well-dressed rabbit, is ideal for experienced stitchers who enjoy three-dimensional work and novelty embellishment. It relies for its appeal on hand appliqué, freezer-paper flowers, and button embellishments.

Finished size: 38½ x 41½in/97.75 x 105.5cm
Skill level: Intermediate

## Materials

- Eight different light-colored backgrounds:
  A: 30 x 7in/76 x 17.5cm
  B: 10 x 46in/25.5 x 117cm
  C: 12 x 12in/30.5 x 30.5cm
  D: 12 x 6in/30.5 x 15.25cm
  E: 14 x 16in/35.5 x 40.5cm
  F: 10 x 10in/25.5 x 25.5cm
  G: 10 x 6in/25.5 x 15.5cm
  H: 10 x 16in/25 x 40cm
- Selection of fabrics 6in/15.25cm square in five colors—green, blue, pink, yellow, brown—with at least four fabrics in each color for the motifs
- Inner border: 8in/20.25cm
- Outer border: ½yd/0.5m
- Binding: ½yd/0.5m

- Cotton perlé No 8 embroidery thread: cream
- Cotton perlé No 5 embroidery thread: light colors, as fabrics
- Six-stranded embroidery thread
- Small buttons: ¼–½in/ 0.75–1.5cm diameter
- 1½in/3.75cm wide bias tape for the curved sunflower stem: 6in/15.25cm
- Five dolls' buttons for eyes
- Freezer paper for the appliqués
- Batting: 41 x 44in/103 x 111cm
- Backing: 41 x 44in/103 x 111cm

- For templates see pages 141–3

## Cutting and Assembling

Read the Techniques chapter for instructions on freezer paper appliqué (*see page 131*).

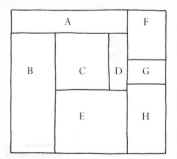

A = Convolvulus  E = Wheelbarrow
B = Sunflower     F = Watering Can
C = Tulip Pot      G = Zinnias
D = Bluebells      H = Rabbit

## Convolvulus Vine (A)

1 Cut one background 23½ x 5½in/59.75 x 14cm.

2 Draw a vine and stems on the background. Chain stitch over the drawn line.

3 Cut 13 freezer-paper leaves. Cut each from fabric ¼in/ 0.75cm larger all around. Arrange and appliqué each so that they hang from the vine.

4 Cut five pink flowers. Turn under ¼in/0.75cm on the curved edge of the flower. Press. With right sides together, fold the flower in half to form a quarter-circle. Stitch down the straight edge.

5 Turn the cone right side out and arrange so that the seam is at the center back. Work gathering stitches close to the curved edge through all the layers. Gather up the stitches loosely and fasten off the thread. Arrange each flower on a stem and appliqué in position.

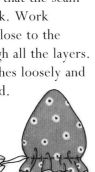

## Sunflowers (B)

1 For X, cut ten squares 3in/7.5cm.
Cut:J: 10½ x 3in/ 26.75 x 7.5cm
K: 20½ x 3in/ 52 x 7.5cm
L: 20½ x 1½in/ 52 x 3.75cm
M: 5½ x 3in/ 14 x 7.5cm
N: 3½ x 9½in/9 x 24cm

| L | M | | J | K |
|---|---|---|---|---|
| | | N | | |
| | X | | | |
| | X | | | |
| | X | | X | |
| | X | | X | |
| | X | | X | |
| | X | | X | |
| | | P | | |

2 From yellow, for the petals, cut 16 squares 3in/7.5cm.

3 For the flower centers, cut two freezer paper circles 3in/7.5cm diameter. Cut ¼in/ 0.75cm larger all around. Cut five

leaves (two units for each). Cut one bee (see page 107).

4 For the stem (P), cut a piece 20½ x 1in/52 x 2.5cm.

5 Appliqué the curved edge of each leaf section to a square. Stitch two squares together to form one leaf. Stitch two leaves together. Stitch J to the top.

6 Stitch the three remaining leaves together to form the right-hand side of the stem. Stitch M to the top.

7 Between the two strips, stitch P. Press. Add K, L, and N following the diagram left.

8 Appliqué the curved bias binding stem in place. Add a bee (see page 107).

9 For the petals, fold each 3in/7.5cm square in half across the diagonal. Find the center of the long edge. Fold in the two corners to this point.

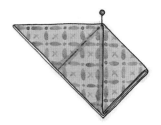

**10** Sew running stitch across the widest point, through all the layers. Gather up the stitches and secure. Trim the excess points away.

**11** Lightly draw the flower center on the background. Arrange eight petals around the circle so that the raw edges will be covered by the flower center. Pin. Appliqué each in position. Appliqué the flower center. Tie buttons to the flower center.

## Tulip Pot (C)

**1** Cut one background 10½ x 11½in/26.75 x 29.25cm.

**2** From freezer paper, cut five hearts, four leaves, one plant pot and rim, one rabbit, and one bee. Cut each from fabric ¼in/0.75cm larger all around.

**3** Appliqué each motif in position, beginning with the leaves, then plant pot, rim, flowers, and rabbit.

**4** Chain stitch each stem. Tie a button to the top of each tulip using six strands of thread. Make a bee, following the instructions on page 107.

**5** Stitch on the rabbit's eye. Stem stitch the whiskers and satin stitch the nose.

## Bluebells (D)

**1** Cut one background 11½ x 4½in/29.25 x 11.5cm.

**2** From freezer paper, cut two leaves. Cut each from fabric ¼in/0.75cm larger all around.

**3** For the bluebells, using shades from dark to light blue, cut eight rectangles 4 x 3in/ 10 x 7.5cm.

**4** At one 4in/10cm edge of each rectangle, turn under a small seam. Sew running stitch across the seam allowance. Gather up the stitches and secure. Fold each rectangle in half, right sides together. Stitch the 3in/7.5cm straight edge.

**5** Turn the bluebell right side out. Turn under a ⅜in/1cm seam at the raw edge and fingerpress. Arrange so that the seam sits at the center back.

**6** Sew running stitch ¼in/ 0.75cm from the bottom of the bell, loosely gather up the threads, and secure the gathers with a small stitch.

**7** Arrange the eight bells with the darkest shades at the bottom and the lightest at the top. Appliqué the bluebells and leaves in position. Chain stitch the stem.

## Wheelbarrow (E)

**1** Cut one background 14½ x 12½in/36.75 x 31.75cm.

**2** From freezer paper, cut one wheelbarrow, six leaves, three bees, and one rabbit. Cut each from fabric ¼in/0.75cm larger all around.

**3** For the flowers, cut eight circles 3½in/9cm in diameter. Cut four small circles 3in/7.5cm in diameter.

**4** Appliqué first the leg of the wheelbarrow, then the barrow, wheel, handle, wheel frame, and the rabbit.

**5** Make the flowers following the instructions for Zinnias (*see step 4*). Position each flower and leaf. Appliqué the leaves, then add the flowers. Sew on the rabbit's eyes and satin stitch the nose.

**Watering Can (F)**

**1** Cut one background 8½ x 9½in/21.5 x 24.25cm.

**2** From freezer paper, cut one watering can, one heart, two leaves, and one bee. Cut each motif from fabric ¼in/0.75cm larger all around.

**3** Appliqué the watering can, then the heart and leaves.

**4** Using embroidery thread, chain stitch the flower stem. Add the bee following the instructions on page 107.

**Zinnias (G)**

**1** Cut one background 8½ x 5½in/ 21.5 x 14cm.

**2** For the flowers, cut two circles 3½in/9cm in diameter.

**3** From freezer paper cut eight leaves. Cut each from fabric ¼in/0.75cm larger all around.

**4** To make the flower heads, turn under ¼in/0.75cm around each circle. Sew running stitch around the outer edge of the seam. Gather the threads and fasten off.

**5** Appliqué four leaves for each stem onto the background. Chain stitch the stem of each flower. Stitch on a circle for each flower head. For decoration, sew a button to each flower center.

**Rabbit (H)**

**1** Cut one background 14½ x 8½in/36.75 x 21.5cm.

**2** From freezer paper, cut the motifs for the rabbit and his clothes. Cut each from fabric ¼in/0.75cm larger all around. Use the reverse of the fabric for the cuffs.

**3** Arrange and appliqué each motif on the background in the following order: feet, front paws, t-shirt, cuffs, dungarees, cuffs, head, label. Overlap the shapes where appropriate.

**4** Stitch on dolls' buttons for eyes. Satin stitch the nose using three strands of brown or black embroidery thread. Stem stitch the whiskers and mouth.

## Bee

1 Appliqué each bee body in the required position.

2 To make the wings, wrap one strand of No 8 perlé embroidery thread around two fingers, five times. Slide thread from your fingers and twist the center. Wrap a length of thread around the twist and knot.

3 Place the wings on the body and stitch a button on the knot using two strands of thread.

## Assembling the Quilt Top

1 Following the quilt plan on page 103, with right sides together and raw edges aligned, stitch C to D. Stitch this unit to the top of E.

2 Stitch B to the left-hand side. Add A across the top.

3 Stitch F to the top of G. Add H to the bottom of G. Stitch the two panels together to complete the quilt top. Press the back of the quilt top.

4 For the inner border, cut four strips 1¾in/4.5cm wide across the width of the fabric.

5 For the outer border, cut four strips 4in/10cm wide across the width of the fabric.

*Above: Detail of rabbit and border.*

6 Attach the inner and outer borders, mitering each corner.

7 Cut and piece 4¾yd/4.4m of 2½in/6.5cm wide fabric for the continuous binding.

8 Make up the quilt sandwich. Bind the quilt and miter the corners to finish.

# Novelty Quilts

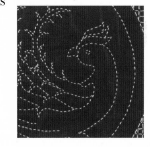

The field of patchwork and quilting is so wide ranging that it will provide something of interest to anyone who is interested in needlework. The quilts in this chapter represent techniques that are difficult to categorize; Silk Fans is as much an embroidered quilt as it is a patchwork quilt, the density of embellishment is reminiscent of crazy quilt patchwork, but the background design has traditional patchwork roots. This quilt will appeal to those who enjoy hand stitching.

The intriguing technique of Cathedral Windows has been used to show novelty fabric to effect, in this appealing small wallhanging suitable for a child's room. For a contemporary look to decorate a modern interior, the Folded Silk Hanging will create an opulent focus. Japanese Sashiko will appeal to those who enjoy hand sewing and want a new challenge.

Whatever your level of ability, there is something in this chapter to inspire the quilter looking for a fresh challenge.

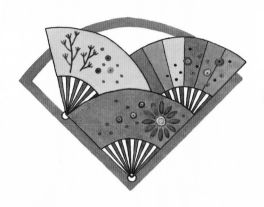

# Silk Fans

Speed-piecing machine techniques are combined with highly decorative hand embroidery stitches on this richly colored miniature silk wallhanging.

Finished size: 23 x 18in/58.5 x 45.75cm
Number of blocks: 12
Finished block: 5 x 5in/13 x 13cm
Skill level: Enthusiastic intermediate with embroidery skills

## Materials

◆ Cream dupion silk: ½yd/0.5m
◆ Coffee dupion silk: ½yd/0.5m
◆ Five different brightly colored silks for the fans: ½yd/0.5m square
◆ Solid color silk for the corners and binding: ½yd/0.5m
◆ Lightweight cotton for the foundations: ½yd/0.5m
◆ Assorted embroidery thread
◆ Small beads and sequins
◆ Backing: 25 x 20in/64 x 51cm
◆ Thin cardboard

◆ For templates see page 137

## Cutting

1 From cream silk, cut six squares each 5⅞in/15cm. Cut the same from coffee silk.

2 From the cotton foundation, cut twelve squares each 7in/ 17.75cm.

3 Make cardboard templates for the fan segment and corner. On the wrong side of the bright silk, draw around the fan. Cut twelve from each color, adding a seam allowance all around. Cut twelve green corners. From different colors, cut four corner posts for the border 2½in/6.5cm square.

4 Cut two cream borders 2 x 20½in/5 x 52cm and two borders 2 x 15½in/5 x 39.25cm.

5 For binding, cut two strips 2½in/6.5cm wide across the width of the fabric. Cross-cut to make two strips 25in/63.5cm long and two strips 20in/ 50.75cm long.

## Making the Background

1 Following the instructions on page 14 for speed-piecing half-square triangles, use the cream and coffee silk squares to make twelve bicolor squares.

2 Center each half-square triangle right side up on a foundation square. Stitch the pieces together within the seam allowance of the silk

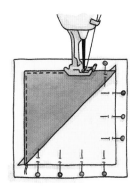

**Making the Fans**

1 Arrange five fan segments—one from each color—in the desired sequence. Stitch the segments together along one long edge. Press.

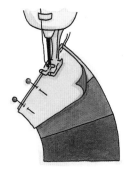

2 Place each fan on a coffee/cream background,

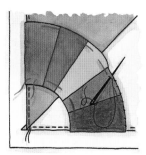

aligning the center of the middle segment with the diagonal seam. Baste.

3 Turn under the top curved edge and hem stitch in place.

4 Position a corner piece at the bottom left-hand side. Turn under the top curved edge and hem stitch as before.

5 Embroider over the seam lines of the fans using decorative stitches—herringbone, feather stitch, cross stitch, lazy daisy, whipped stitch, and French knots. Add beads and sequins as desired. (Avoid pressing sequins or plastic beads as they melt.)

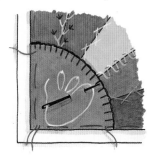

**Assembling the Quilt Top**

1 Trim the excess foundation away from each block. Arrange the blocks as desired into the quilt top.

2 Stitch the blocks into rows. Stitch the rows together.

3 Embroider the seam lines joining the blocks.

4 Add a long border to each side of the quilt top. To each end of the shorter borders add a corner post. Embroider a motif on each corner post. Stitch the shorter borders across the top and bottom.

5 Center the quilt top on top of the backing. Trim the backing to the same size as the quilt top. Baste together in a grid 4in/10cm apart.

6 Tie-quilt the top to the backing at the corner of each fan block.

7 Bind the quilt to finish and miter the corners.

*Opposite: Close-up detail of the fans, showing the embroidered seam lines with applied beads and sequins.*

# Cathedral Windows

Cathedral windows provide an ideal opportunity
to use novelty fabrics in small quantities. Some windows have
been filled with a solid medium blue to contrast with
the busy teddy bear fabric.

Finished size: 15 x 15in/38 x 38cm
Number of blocks: 16
Finished block: 2½ x 2½in/6.5 x 6.5cm
Skill level: Confident intermediate

## Materials

◆ Novelty teddy bear print:
½yd/0.5m
◆ Dark blue solid: ¾yd/0.7m
◆ Medium blue solid:
¼yd/0.25m
◆ Backing: 17in/43cm square
◆ Batting: 17in/43cm square

## Cutting

**1** For the background of the cathedral windows, from dark blue, cut 16 squares each 6in/15.25cm.

**2** In the center of a piece of cardboard, mark and cut a window 1¾in/4.5cm. Use the window to determine which features to cut from the teddy

bear print. Mark and cut 18 squares with novelty centers.

**3** From the teddy print, cut four borders 2½ x 11in/6.5 x 28cm.

**4** For the cathedral windows, from medium blue, cut six squares 1¾in/4.5cm. Cut four border corner posts each 2½in/6.5cm square.

**5** From batting, cut two strips 2½ x 11in/6.5 x 28cm. Also cut two strips 2½ x 14in/6.5 x 35.5cm.

**6** For the binding, from dark blue, cut and piece a length 2½ x 62in/6.5 x 157.5cm.

## Making the Blocks

1 To make the background, fold each dark blue square in half, right sides together.

2 Stitch the short edges together. Snip the corners.

3 Press open the seams. Refold the pieces, pinning the seams together at the open side.

4 By hand or machine, stitch across the remaining raw edge leaving a small gap in the seam through which to turn the square right side out.

5 Clip the corners of the seams and press open.

6 Turn the square right side out and ease the corners out. Press flat.

7 Find the center of the square. Fold each corner in to the centre. Secure with stitches. The folded side is the right side.

8 Place two squares right sides together. Whipstitch along one edge. Make a background, four squares wide and four deep.

9 Pin the teddy and medium blue 1¾in/4.5cm windows in place over the join of two background blocks.

10 Turn the folded edges of the background over the raw edges of the window. Stab stitch in place.

## Borders

1 To give a more padded effect, line each shorter border with batting and machine-stitch ¼in/0.75cm from one long raw edge.

2 Fingerpress the seam allowance to the wrong side. With right sides together, whip-stitch the border to the quilt centre, ensuring the stitching is as invisible as possible.

3 Machine-stitch a medium blue corner to each end of the longer borders.

4 Repeat steps 1 and 2 to add the remaining borders to the quilt top.

5 Place the quilt top onto the backing. Secure the layers together with a small cross-stitch at the center of each cathedral window square.

6 Sew a layer of permanent basting around the outer raw edges, within the seam allowance and through all the layers.

7 Bind the quilt with double fold binding. Miter the corners as you work.

# Picnic Rug

Simple-style appliqué and tied quilting using novelty popcorn balls and crow's feet provide the focus of attention for this easy-to-make throw.

Finished size: 36 x 36in/91.5 x 91.5cm
Number of blocks: 9
Finished block: 8 x 8in/20.5 x 20.5cm
Skill level: Beginner

## Materials

- Red gingham: ½yd/0.5m
- Berry print: 1yd/1m
- Solid green: ½yd/0.5m
- Solid red: ¼yd/0.25m
- Scraps of fusible webbing
- DMC perlé cotton No 8 in the following colors:
  666 for the crow's feet on the gingham
  319 for the tied quilting on the berry print and outer border
  369 for the popcorn balls and crow's feet on the inner border
- DMC stranded cotton: shade 369 for the popcorn balls
- Backing: 38in/97cm square
- Batting: 38in/97cm square

- For template see page 143

## Cutting

1 From gingham, cut nine squares 6in/15.25cm.

2 From the berry print, cut five squares 7in/17.75cm. Cut each in half across both diagonals to yield 20 triangles. For the outer border, cut two strips 4½ x 28½in/11.5 x 72.5cm and two strips 4½ x 36½in/11.5 x 92.75cm.

3 From solid green, cut four squares 7in/17.75cm. Divide each as before into four triangles—16 in total. For the

inner border, cut two strips 2½ x 24½in/6.5 x 62.25cm, and two strips 2½ x 28½in/6.5 x 72.5cm. For the binding, cut and piece a continuous length 2½in x 4¼yd/6.5 x 3.9m.

4 Trace the heart pattern on page 143. Stick the tracing to thin cardboard and cut out.

5 Bond scraps of fusible webbing to the wrong side of the solid red following the manufacturer's instructions. On the paper side of the web, draw nine heart shapes, leaving at least ½in/1.5cm between each. Cut out the hearts.

## Making the Blocks

1 Stitch a berry print triangle to opposite sides of five gingham squares. Stitch two triangles to the remaining opposite sides. Press.

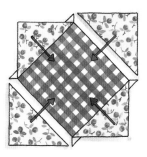

2 Repeat, stitching the solid green triangles to the remaining gingham squares.

3 Fuse a red heart to the center of each red gingham square, following the manufacturer's instructions for working with fusible webbing.

4 With red embroidery thread, work blanket stitch around the outer edge of each heart.

5 Arrange the blocks into the quilt top—three across and three down, alternating the solid and print blocks.

6 Stitch the blocks together into rows, then into the quilt top, taking care not to stretch the bias edges of the blocks.

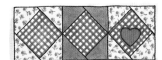

7 Stitch a short green border to opposite sides of the quilt. Trim the ends even with the quilt top. Add the long borders to the quilt top and bottom. Press.

8 Repeat to add the outer borders to the quilt.

## Finishing

1 Make up the quilt sandwich and baste the layers together using a 4in/10cm grid.

2 Tie-quilt the berry border and triangles with green perlé thread (*see page 27*).

3 Add crow's feet quilting to the red gingham squares with red thread and to the green inner border with cream thread.

4 Add popcorn balls to the green triangles.

5 Bind the quilt and miter the corners, following the instructions on page 131.

*Left: Detail of the heart motif.*

# Folded Silk Hanging

Strips of silk are pieced together to form the background of this attractive wallhanging. Folded prairie points and rectangles of silk in contrasting shades of dupion silk add another dimension to the quilt surface.

Finished size: 22 x 27in/56 x 68.75cm
Skill level: Intermediate

## Materials

- Mustard dupion silk: ½yd/0.5m
- Red dupion silk: ½yd/0.5m
- Cream dupion silk: ½yd/0.5m
- Green dupion silk for the project and for the binding: ½yd/0.5m
- Rust dupion silk: ½yd/0.5m
- Backing: 24 x 29in/61 x 74cm
- Batting: 24 x 29in/61 x 74cm

*Follow the quilt plan above and refer to the photograph on page 120.*

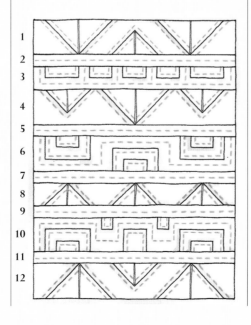

## Cutting and Piecing

Cut each piece as you require it. The raw edges of the prairie points and the rectangles are trapped in the seams as the rows are stitched together.

## Rows 1 and 2

1 From mustard, cut one piece 18½ x 3½in/47 x 9cm.

2 From green, cut one square 3¼in/9cm for the prairie points.

**3** From rust, cut two squares 4½in/11.5cm for the prairie points.

**4** For the prairie points, fold each square in half, wrong sides together. Press. Find the center of the long raw edge.

**5** Fold in the corners diagonally to the marked center point to make a triangle. Press. Baste the center front opening of the triangle shut. This is the right side.

**6** Align the center point of the raw edges of the green prairie point with the center of a long side of mustard. Align raw edges. Baste in place.

**7** Put the rust prairie points aside until the whole quilt top is assembled.

**8** From red, for row 2 cut one piece 18½ x 1½in/47 x 3.75cm. Stitch row 2 to row 1.

## Row 3

**1** From cream, for the background, cut one piece 18½ x 2½in/47 x 6.5cm.

**2** From rust, cut three squares 2½in/6.5cm, and two rectangles 3½ x 2½in/9 x 6.5cm. Fold each rectangle and square in half, right sides together. Pin.

**3** Working from the folded edge, stitch down the two opposite sides. Clip the corners. Turn right side out. Press.

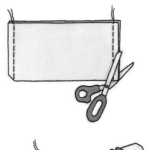

**4** For row 3, baste two large and three small rust rect-

angles to one long edge of row 3, spacing them at equal intervals. Place the two outer ones 1in/2.5cm from the outer edges. Stitch row 3 to row 2.

## Rows 4 and 5

**1** From green, cut one piece 18½ x 3½in/47 x 9cm.

**2** From red, cut one square 4½in/11.5cm and two squares 3¼in/9cm for the prairie points. Make the prairie points.

**3** Position the small prairie points 1in/2.5cm from each short edge of the green on one long side. Center the large prairie point on the same side. Baste in place. Stitch row 4 to row 3.

**4** From mustard, for row 5, cut one piece 18½ x 1½in/ 47 x 3.75cm. Stitch row 5 to 4.

## Rows 6 and 7

**1** From rust, cut one piece 18½ x 3½in/47 x 9cm.

**2** From cream, cut three squares 4½in/11.5cm for the rectangles. Make as before.

3 From green, cut three squares 2½in/6.5cm for the rectangles. Make as before.

4 Baste the rectangles in place. Stitch row 6 to row 5.

5 From red, for row 7, cut one piece 18½ x 1½in/47 x 3.75cm. Carefully stitch row 7 to row 6.

## Rows 8 and 9

1 From cream, cut one piece 18½ x 2½in/47 x 6.5cm.

2 From mustard, cut three 3¼in/9cm squares for the prairie points. Make as before, then baste to the bottom edge of row 8. Stitch row 7 to row 8.

3 From green, for row 9, cut one piece 18½ x 1½in/47 x 3.75cm. Stitch row 9 to row 8.

## Rows 10 and 11

1 From red, cut one piece 18½ x 3½in/47 x 9cm.

2 From rust, cut two squares 2½in/6.5cm. Make as before.

3 From cream, cut two squares 4½in/11.5cm. Cut one rectangle 2½ x 4½in/6.5 x 11.5cm, and two rectangles 2½ x 1½in/6.5 x 3.75cm. Make as before. Place on the background.

4 Baste three larger cream rectangles and two rust rectangles along the bottom edge. Stitch row 10 to row 9.

5 From mustard, for row 11, cut one piece 18½ x 1½in/47 x 3.75cm. Stitch row 11 to row 10.

## Row 12

1 From rust, cut one piece 18½ x 3½in/47 x 9cm.

2 From cream, cut one square 3¼in/9cm for the prairie point. Make as before.

3 From green, cut two squares 4½in/11.5cm for the prairie points. Make as before. Set aside.

4 Baste the cream prairie point to one long edge. Stitch row 12 to row 11.

5 Baste two green prairie points to the bottom edge of row 12 and the two rust prairie points to the top of row 1.

## Finishing

1 Press and trim the edges of the quilt straight. Make up the quilt sandwich. Baste a grid 4in/10cm apart.

2 To prevent the edges of the silk from fraying while the work is quilted, fold the edges of the backing fabric over the raw edges of the quilt top and baste.

3 Handquilt the design by contour quilting the strips, rectangles, and squares.

4 From green, piece a length of binding 110 x 2½in/2.8m x 6.5cm. Bind to finish.

*Below: Detail of a prairie point.*

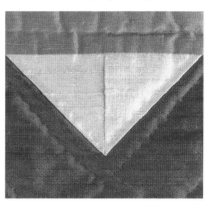

# Japanese Sashiko

Sashiko is traditionally worked using a thick white thread on an indigo blue ground. These small running stitches are neat and even, with the same number of stitches worked on the same part of the pattern throughout.

Finished size: 20 x 20 in/50.75 x 50.75cm
Skill level: Intermediate

## Materials

- Navy cotton chintz: 20in/51cm square
- Blue and white check for binding: ½yd/0.5m square
- Perlé cotton No 8 in white
- Dressmaker's carbon
- Backing: 20in/51cm square
- Flannelette sheeting for batting: 20in/51cm square

- For template see page 127 and enlarge to 18in/45.75cm square.

## Assembling the Quilt

1 Make up the quilt sandwich, using the sheeting in place of batting.

2 Baste a 2in/5cm grid over the quilt surface.

3 Enlarge the design and trace it onto thin paper.

4 Place the dressmaker's carbon, carbon side down, on top of the quilt sandwich. Place the pattern on top. Using a sharp pencil, retrace the design lines onto the fabric.

5 Using one strand of white perlé cotton, handquilt the design. Begin working from the

center of the design. If the design lines become faint, refresh with a quilter's silver pencil.

6 For the grid patterns, work the stitching in logical, continuous lines. Where multiple lines of stitching meet, for example at the center of the *Shippou* (circular border) design, the stitching should appear to radiate out from the center, like flower petals.

7 Cut and piece a length of binding 2½ x 86in/6.5 x 219cm. Bind the quilt, mitering the corners as you work.

*Left: Detail showing center motif, in-fill design and Shippou.*

# Techniques

### Choosing Fabrics

Many of the quilts in this book require only small amounts of fabric. By saving scraps from larger projects you will soon have the beginnings of a collection to form the basis for small quilts.

When buying fabrics, choose the best quality you can afford for good results. One hundred percent quality cotton dressweight will resist fraying, hold a crease well, and prevent the batting seeping through the quilt top. Suppliers are happy to cut small amounts and selection packs of small pieces are often available. If you plan to recycle old fabrics into quilts, cut out any worn or faded areas. Different weights of fabric may cause uneven wear in a quilt. Lighter fabric can be stabilized and strengthened by applying a lightweight interfacing to the back.

Most fabrics produced for patchwork are 44in/112cm wide. For small projects fat quarters are useful. These measure 22 x 18in/ 56 x 46cm and are a more useful shape than the long quarter.

It is important to have a range of both color and value (dark, medium, and light tones), including a variety of solid colors and patterned fabrics. Consider the scale of any patterned fabric in relation to working small—florals, polka dots, plaids, and stripes on a small scale will all work well. A bag of scrap fabrics is an invaluable resource, as many small quilts require minimal amounts.

### Fabric Preparation

Always wash fabrics before beginning any new project. This will remove residual dye and any chemicals and prevent later shrinkage. To wash small amounts of fabric, place in a large jar with a lid, add warm water and a small amount of laundry detergent and shake, then leave to soak for about 20 minutes. Rinse until the water runs clear. Iron while still damp. If dye loss occurs, a solution of one part white vinegar to three parts cold water added to the rinsing water may help to fix the dye. Cut off the corner at one of the selvage edges to prevent threads from unraveling.

Before beginning a project, read through the instructions and study the diagrams. Cut out the largest pieces first. The fabric left over can be used to cut out smaller pieces.

### Batting

The variety of batting types can be confusing for a beginner. Battings are made from natural (cotton, wool, silk) or manmade (polyester) materials, sometimes in combinations of natural and manmade fibers. Each type of batting is good for a specific project.

- "Low-loft" is good for small wallhangings and mini quilts.
- Polyester batting is fine for crib quilts, which need frequent laundering, and for large wallhangings. For full-size bed quilts, large pieces of polyester batting are available to avoid the need to join pieces.
- Cotton batting, which is heavier in weight, will hang well.

## Equipment

Much of the equipment necessary for patchwork is the same as that for dressmaking—scissors, pins, needles, threads, thimble, tape measure, seam ripper, and sewing machine are all standard. Add to these a rotary cutting set and you will be set up to begin.

## Using a Rotary Cutter

Fold the fabric in half with the selvages together, then fold again. Smooth the layers together and press, then place the fabric on the board with the double fold at the front nearest to you. Position the ruler on the fabric with one of the horizontal grid lines of the ruler even with the double fold. Slide the ruler to the edge of the fabric, making sure that the fold and horizontal grid line on the ruler are aligned. Holding the ruler down firmly, push the edge of the cutter along the edge of the ruler away from you to make the first cut, trimming and straightening the edges.

When the fabric has been straightened, it can be cut into strips, squares, rectangles, and triangles by using either the grid on the cutting mat or the ruler.

To use the grid on the mat, position the fabric in line with the grid lines, both vertical and horizontal, and cut the required sizes by lining up the ruler with the measurements on the mat.

For small pieces use the grid on the ruler. This is more accurate, because the ruler grips the fabric. Align the appropriate measurement line on the ruler with the cut edge of the fabric, trapping the pieces to be cut under the ruler, and cut. When using this method, the bulk of the fabric should be on the right if you are right-handed and on the left if you are left-handed.

To rotary-cut bias strips, use a right-angled triangle (set square) to establish the true bias by positioning one of the short sides of the triangle along the crosswise grain. Extend the line along the diagonal edge with a long ruler and use this as a guide when cutting. Cut strips the desired width across the piece. Join bias strips with an angled seam.

## Templates

Templates can be made from cardboard or template plastic. To make a template, trace the pattern provided. Cut out the tracing and stick to thin cardboard. For a motif that will be reused, work with template plastic and follow the manufacturer's instructions.

## Sewing Techniques

Unless otherwise specified in the pattern instructions (eg, the foundation-pieced projects), fabrics are placed right sides together and stitched with a running stitch. The ¼in/0.75cm seam allowance is standard and is included in the measurements.

If your machine does not measure an accurate ¼in/0.75cm seam from the needle to the edge of the presser foot, draw an exact ¼in/0.75cm line from the edge of a piece of paper with a sharp pencil. Place this under the presser foot and lower the needle into the line. Put the presser foot down to make sure that the paper is straight, then stick a strip of narrow masking tape to the bed of the machine so that it meets the edge of the paper. When stitching, guide the raw edges of the fabrics against the edge of the masking tape.

Various techniques for speed-piecing are outlined in the individual instructions. As many involve sewing fabrics together, then cutting across these stitching lines, machine-piecing is recommended. Set your machine so that the stitch is slightly smaller than usual so it is less likely to come undone at the cutting points.

## Chain-piecing

Chain-piecing can speed up the process when you have identical seams to sew. Feed the pairs of pieces through the sewing machine without cutting the threads between them. Lay out the pieces for the blocks on a flat surface to check the overall design. First join small units such as triangles into squares, then squares into strips before joining strips into blocks. Sew in straight lines wherever possible—this is easier than setting pieces into a corner. Establish a sequence for making a block then continue with it for all the blocks in the same pattern.

## Handpiecing

Although machine-piecing is recommended, these quilts can be hand pieced using traditional methods. Make templates for odd shapes. Place each on the wrong side of the fabric and draw

around each template. This is the stitching line, so remember to leave enough space between the pieces for the seam allowances. Check as you mark that the straight grain of the fabric will be parallel with the sides of the block. Cut out the pieces with sharp scissors.

Arrange the block in the correct sequence on a flat surface. Place the pieces right sides together and pin, with marked stitching lines matching up. Use a neat running stitch with the occasional backstitch to strengthen the seam. Check that the lines match by looking on the back of the work. The stitching should start and end with each seam line, leaving seam allowances free. If handpiecing, press seams to the darker side if possible and, where there are multiple fabrics meeting in one point, the seams can be spiralled to reduce bulk.

## Appliqué

Appliqué is the process of stitching cut-out shapes to a background fabric; the background may be one whole piece or a patchwork of pieces. All the appliqué quilts in this book use speed techniques.

## Appliqué Using Fusible Webbing

Fusible webbing is mounted onto paper and is used to adhere one fabric to another. This is a fast method of appliqué, and manufacturers claim that once bonded in place, the fabric does not need further stitching. However, all appliqué shapes have been decorated with a satin stitch or buttonhole embellishment so that the raw edges of the fabrics are not visible. Place the webbing paper side up and iron the paper side of the webbing onto the wrong side of the fabric to be applied. Draw the shape required onto the paper, drawing freehand or using a template. Cut out the shape with the paper still attached, then peel away the paper. Position the appliqué shape, webbing side down, on the background in the required position. Apply heat with the iron and the two fabrics will stick together. For this method of appliqué, where you will use either machine satin stitch or buttonhole stitch to cover the raw edge of the applied fabric, there is no need to add turnings.

The process of working machine satin stitch can cause the

fabric layers to pucker, giving disappointing results. The problem can be rectified by placing tearaway stabilizer behind the work before stitching. Pin a large enough piece behind the work and sew through all layers —the background, appliqué, and stabilizer. Tear away the stabilizer when the stitching is complete.

## Appliqué Using Freezer Paper

Freezer paper appliqué will appeal to those who enjoy hand work. This is a traditional form of appliqué, only here the shapes are "molded" around a freezer paper template to help them keep their shape. From the pattern pieces, make a same-size freezer paper template for each shape. Cut out the fabric, adding a ¼in/0.75cm seam allowance all around. Iron the waxy side of the freezer paper to the wrong side of the fabric, so that the two "stick" together. Use the crisp lines of the edge of the freezer paper as a guide and fingerpress the fabric seam allowance underneath. Position the shape on the background and stitch in place, taking care not to catch the freezer paper in the stitching. Remove the paper

before making the final stitches.

## Borders

Borders can be simple strips to frame the quilt, or pieced to complement the overall design. They should contain and balance the body of the quilt and deserve as much thought and planning. Typical pieced patterns are "sawtooth" (see Autumn Leaves, Flying Geese and squares set as diamonds). Straight borders can be "square-ended" with corner posts or mitered.

For straight-cut borders, allow a little extra in both length and width and trim as you work—this will give a more expert finish. For corner posts cut four squares, the same measurement as the width of the border strips. Add these to each end of two borders.

When your quilt top is complete, snip off all thread ends, and press seams on the back and the front.

## Mitered Borders

To accommodate the miter, each end of the border pieces must extend beyond the corner of the quilt by at least the width of the

border; allow more if possible.

To form the miter: Join the borders to the edges of the quilt beginning and ending ¼in/ 0.75cm from the beginning and end of the length of the quilt top. At each end, fingerpress the seam allowance under or the miter will be distorted. Fold the quilt top diagonally in half, placing the outer edges of the border strips together. Across the border, draw a line at an exact 45° angle joining the outer corner of the border to the corner of the quilt top where the stitching between the border and quilt top meet. Stitch along the marked line. Check the fit of the border, then cut away the excess border fabric. Press the border seams open, then press the border seams toward the border. Press again on the right side.

## Marking the Quilting Design

Use a fabric marker that will make a fine line and can be easily removed after use. For light-colored fabrics, a well-sharpened pencil with a hard lead will make a line fine enough to be covered by the stitching. For dark fabrics, use a well-sharpened silver or white pencil. Other options are the chalk wheel dispenser, which will make very fine lines that can be brushed away, dressmaker's carbon paper and a tracing wheel, or a sliver of soap.

Straight lines and grids can be marked with narrow masking tape. Stitch against the edge and remove the tape as soon as you can to avoid leaving a residue.

Contour quilting—lines that follow the patterns in the patch-work and quilting in-the-ditch (lines of stitching buried in the seam)—need not be marked. This is also true of freehand quilting either with the feed-dog dropped or engaged.

## Quilt Layers

The definition of a quilt is that it must have three layers. On a flat surface, place the backing wrong side up, then the batting and finally the quilt top right side up to make a sandwich of the three layers. Pin the layers together. The backing and batting should be slightly larger all around the outside edges. With small pieces of work, it is tempting to skip the basting process and begin quilting straight away. However, even with small pieces there is still a danger of puckers developing on

the back, so it is worth spending the extra time basting the layers together. Baste in a grid about 4in/10cm apart, then baste around the outer edges.

## Quilting

The quilting stitch is a small running stitch that is both functional and decorative. The quilting stitch holds the three layers of the quilt together and needs to be of a scale to fit the size of your mini-quilt. This is often easier to achieve with machine stitching.

## Handquilting

Small quilts can be quilted in the lap, but hoops or frames help to maintain tension evenly. To work the edges of a small quilt in a hoop, baste extensions—broad strips of fabric—evenly to the sides, so that they can be contained in the hoop. Use a fine needle (8, 9 or 10 "betweens"). Working with a single strand of a good-quality quilting thread, knot the end and take a stitch into the middle layer an inch/few centi-meters from where you will start to quilt. Come up through the

quilting line and, with a tug on the thread, pop the knot into the middle layer to conceal it. Quilt from the center out to avoid trapping puckers as you work. Use a thimble to protect your middle finger as you push the needle through the layers. Make sure that each stitch goes through to the back every time. Take small, even running stitches. Practice the "rocker motion," which is a way of pivoting the needle to pick up several stitches at once in a technique that, once learned, will result in smooth, even stitches.

To finish a length of thread, tie a couple of small knots close to the surface of the fabric and pop the end into the center layer, clipping off the thread end.

## Machine-Quilting

A walking foot is a useful attachment to evenly feed the layers of the quilt through the machine. Another method of machine quilting is "free-motion" quilting. This method requires you to guide the work—imagine you are drawing with a pencil (the machine needle), but instead of moving the pencil you are moving the paper (the work to be quilted). By dropping the feed-dog on the machine, work can be guided in any direction.

## Double-fold Straight Separate Binding

A narrow folded binding made using a double thickness of fabric makes a neat finish. Cut strips of binding fabric 2–2½in/5–6.5cm wide on the straight grain of the fabric. If strips need to be joined, a diagonal seam will be less visible and reduce bulk. Cut two each for the length and width of the quilt top. Allow a little extra for tidying the ends of the third and fourth strips. Trim excess batting and backing even with the quilt top.

Fold the binding strips in half lengthways, wrong sides innermost. Pin the folded binding strips to the right side of the quilt, with raw edges even and the fold toward the center of the quilt. Machine-stitch through all the layers. Fold the binding to the backing side and slipstitch in place, concealing the machine stitching. On the second and third sides of the quilt, tidy each end of the binding strip by sewing the short ends together, right sides innermost. Trim the seam

and turn through before applying these strips to the quilt top. Continue the hemming stitches along the corners.

For a quick machine binding, stitch binding strips to the wrong side of the quilt, fold over to the right side, and machine down. Tidy the ends of the third and fourth strips.

## Bias Binding

Bias binding will use more fabric but it is easier to miter and useful to accommodate curved corners and scallops because it will stretch. To make a continuous length of bias binding, take a 12in/30.5cm square of fabric, fold one corner down to form a diagonal crease, then cut in half along the foldline to yield two triangles. With right sides facing, stitch the two triangles together along one short straight edge. Use small stitches. Press the seam open. On the wrong side of the fabric draw parallel lines the required width apart along the bias edges. With right sides together, pin and stitch the straight grain edges of the fabric, offsetting the ends of the seam by the width of the bias strip and matching the

drawn lines. Press the seam open. Cut continuous strips of bias binding from the resulting cylinder of fabric along the marked lines. Fold the binding in half with the seams inside, handling it carefully so as not to stretch the fabric.

## To Miter the Corners of Bias Binding

Begin to apply the binding in the center of one side and begin stitching it down approximately 2in/5cm from the corner. Stitch up to the first corner, stopping ¼in/0.75cm short of the edge. Take one or two backstitches and break the threads. At the corner fold the binding up at a 90° angle and press the crease. Fold the binding down to lie alongside the next side and pin. Continue to stitch the binding to the quilt top. Repeat for the three remaining corners. When the binding is attached all around the edges join the two ends by lapping the fold at the start over the raw edge at the other end of the binding strip. As you hem the binding over onto the wrong side of the quilt a folded miter will be formed on the front by the crease.

133

# Templates

All templates are actual size

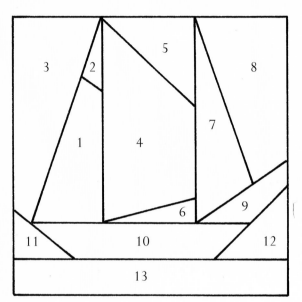

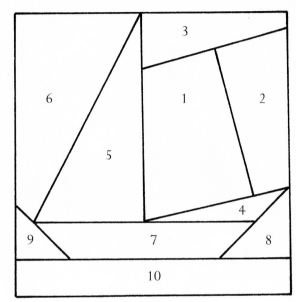

**Plain Sailing (actual size)**

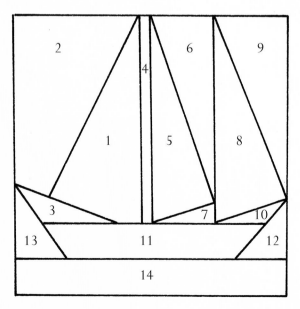

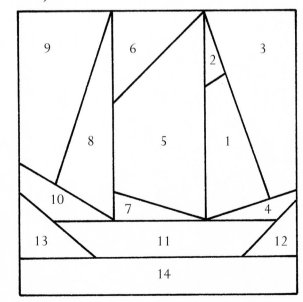

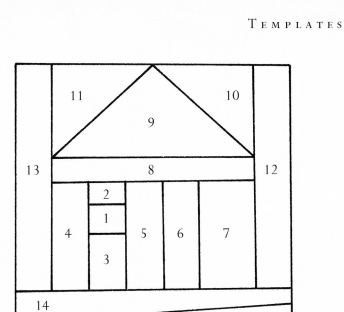

**Plain Sailing**

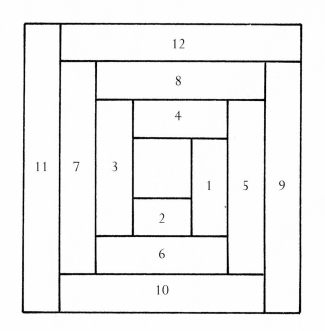

**All actual size**

**Log Cabin Barn Raising**

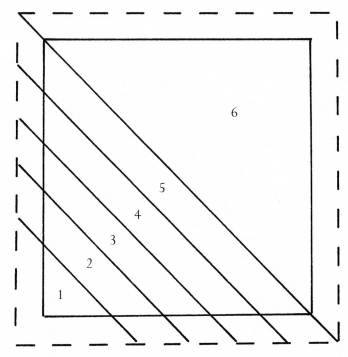

**Roman Stripe**

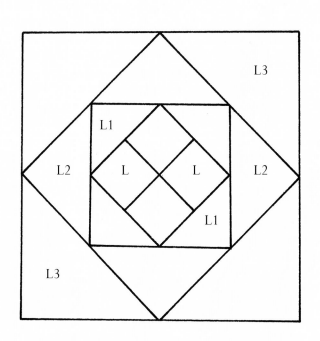

**Snail Trail**

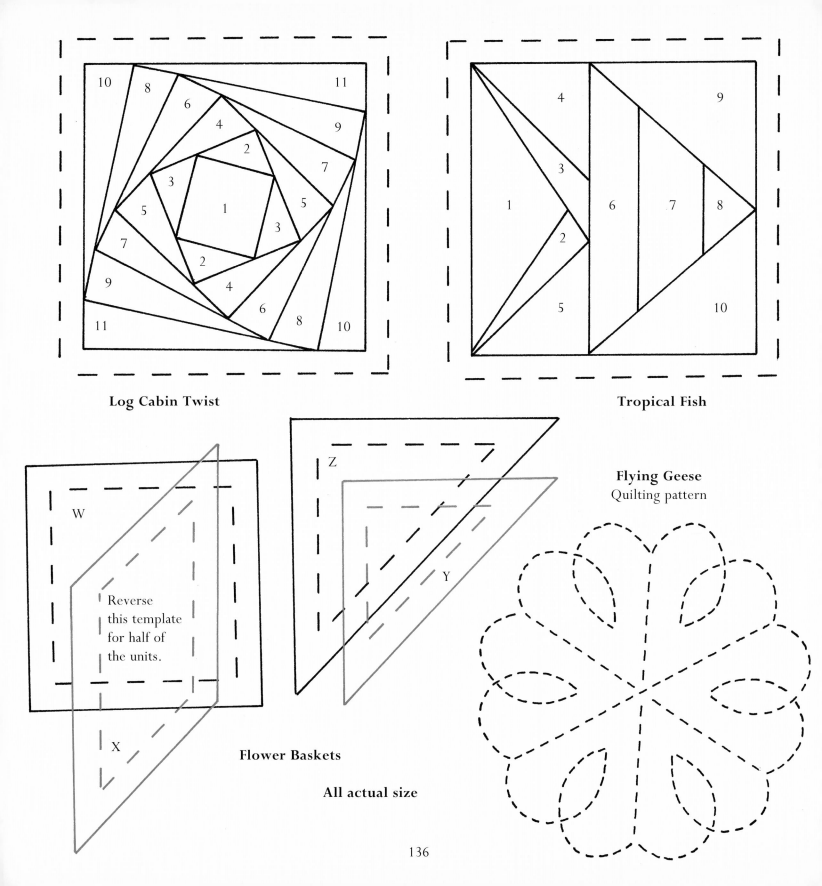

**Log Cabin Twist**

**Tropical Fish**

**Flying Geese**
Quilting pattern

Reverse
this template
for half of
the units.

**Flower Baskets**

**All actual size**

**Mola Quilt**

**All actual size**

**Flying Geese**
Quilting patterns

**Silk Fans**

Fan segment

Fan Corner

137

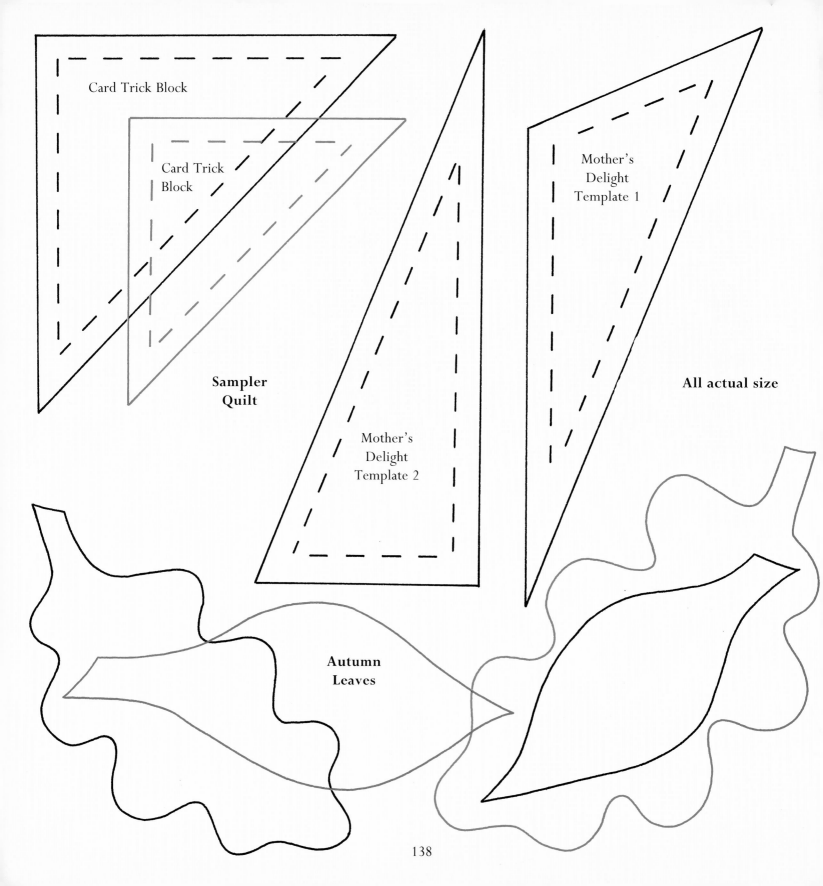

Card Trick Block

Card Trick
Block

**Sampler
Quilt**

Mother's
Delight
Template 2

Mother's
Delight
Template 1

**All actual size**

**Autumn
Leaves**

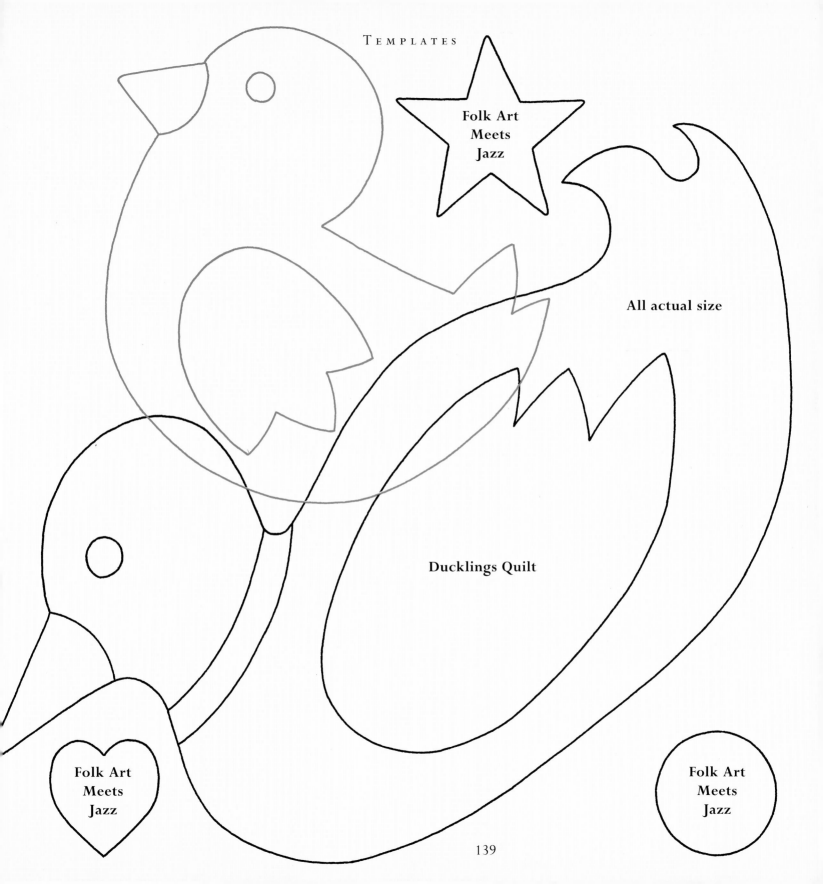

Folk Art
Meets
Jazz

All actual size

Ducklings Quilt

Folk Art
Meets
Jazz

Folk Art
Meets
Jazz

139

Moon

**All actual size**

Reindeer

*Bead*

**Christmas Quilt**

Large tree

Small star
*Use this star for
quilting guide*

Large star

Small tree

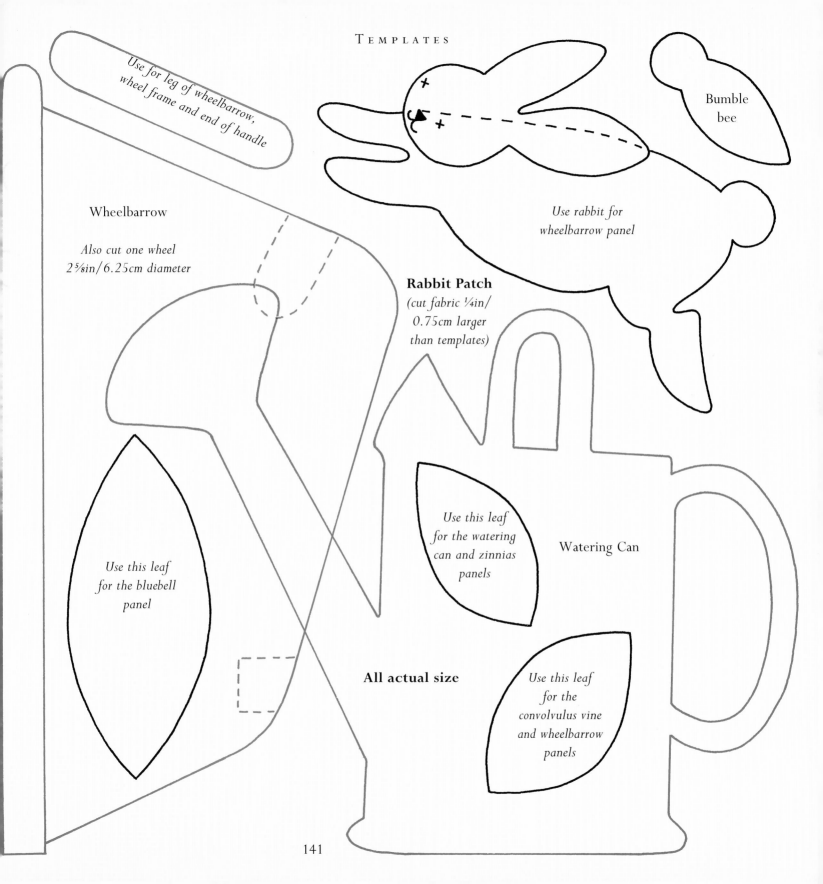

Use for leg of wheelbarrow, wheel frame and end of handle

Bumble bee

Wheelbarrow

*Also cut one wheel 2⅝in/6.25cm diameter*

Use rabbit for wheelbarrow panel

**Rabbit Patch**
*(cut fabric ¼in/ 0.75cm larger than templates)*

*Use this leaf for the bluebell panel*

*Use this leaf for the watering can and zinnias panels*

Watering Can

**All actual size**

*Use this leaf for the convolvulus vine and wheelbarrow panels*

141

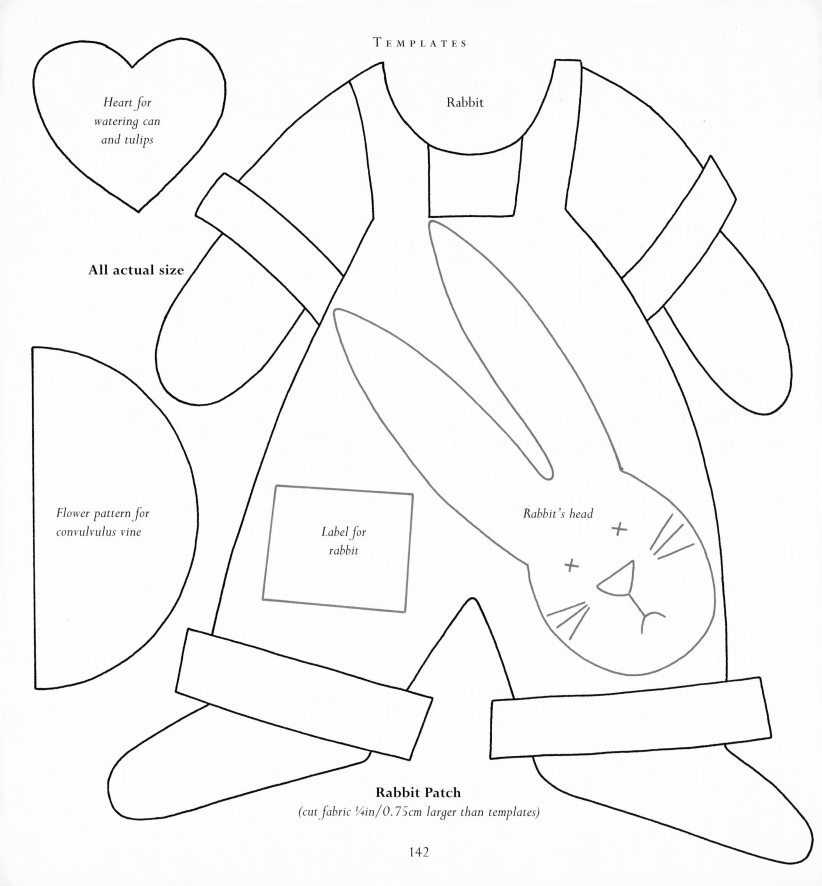

*Heart for
watering can
and tulips*

Rabbit

**All actual size**

*Flower pattern for
convulvulus vine*

*Label for
rabbit*

*Rabbit's head*

**Rabbit Patch**
*(cut fabric ¼in/0.75cm larger than templates)*

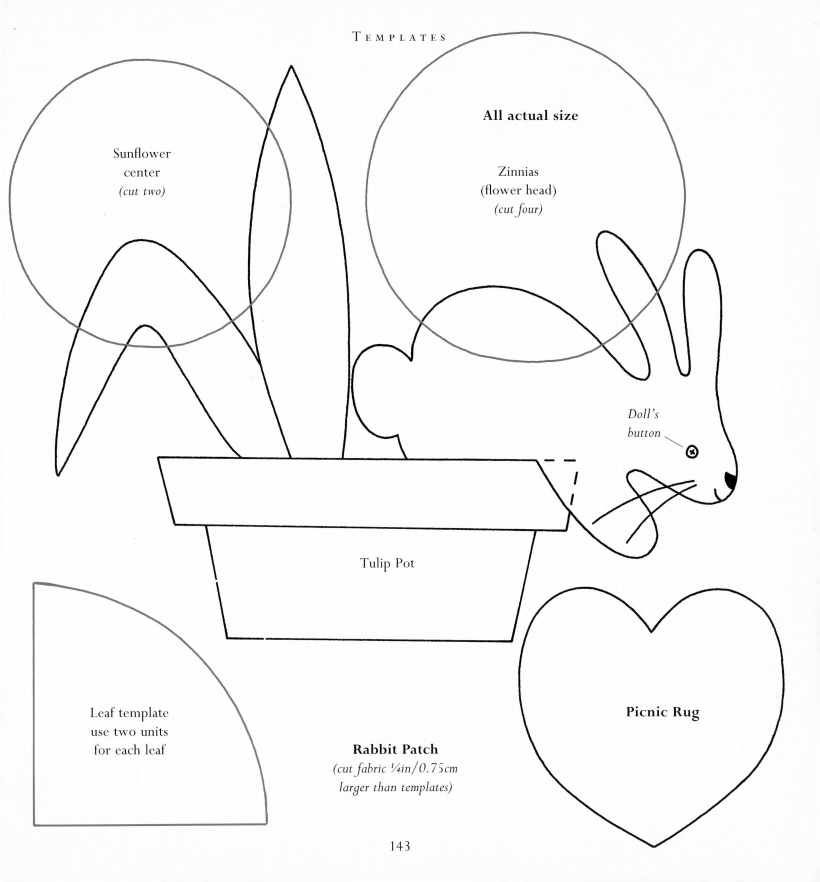

Sunflower
center
*(cut two)*

**All actual size**

Zinnias
(flower head)
*(cut four)*

*Doll's
button*

Tulip Pot

Leaf template
use two units
for each leaf

**Rabbit Patch**
*(cut fabric ¼in/0.75cm
larger than templates)*

**Picnic Rug**

# Index